Economic Integration and the Environment

NEW HORIZONS IN ENVIRONMENTAL ECONOMICS

General Editors: Wallace E. Oates, *Professor of Economics, University of Maryland, USA* and Henk Folmer, *Professor of Economics, Wageningen Agricultural University, The Netherlands and Professor of Environmental Economics, Tilburg University, The Netherlands*

This important series is designed to make a significant contribution to the development of the principles and practices of environmental economics. It includes both theoretical and empirical work. International in scope, it addresses issues of current and future concern in both East and West and in developed and developing countries.

The main purpose of the series is to create a forum for the publication of high quality work and to show how economic analysis can make a contribution to understanding and resolving the environmental problems confronting the world in the late twentieth century.

Recent titles in the series include:

Economic Integration and the Environment
A Political–Economic Perspective
Rolf Bommer

Public Choice and Environmental Regulation
Tradable Permit Systems in the United States
and CO_2 Taxation in Europe
Gert Tinggaard Svendsen

Environmental Policy Analysis with Limited Information
Principles and Applications of the Transfer Method
William H. Desvousges, F. Reed Johnson and H. Spencer Banzhaf

Environmental Transition in Nordic and Baltic Countries
Edited by Hans Aage

Biodiversity, Conservation and Sustainable Development
Principles and Practices with Asian Examples
Clem Tisdell

Green Taxes
Economic Theory and Empirical Evidence from Scandinavia
Edited by Runar Brännlund and Ing-Marie Gren

The Political Economy of Environmental Policy
A Public Choice Approach to Market Institutions
Bouwe R. Dijkstra

The Economic Valuation of Landscape Change
Theory and Policies for Land Use and Conservation
José Manuel L. Santos

Sustaining Development
Environmental Resources in Developing Countries
Daniel W. Bromley

Designing Effective Environmental Regimes
The Key Conditions
Jørgen Wettestad

Economic Integration and the Environment

A Political–Economic Perspective

Rolf Bommer

Economist, Landeszentralbank im Freistaat Bayern, Munich, Germany

NEW HORIZONS IN ENVIRONMENTAL ECONOMICS

Edward Elgar
Cheltenham, UK • Northampton, MA, USA

Published by
Edward Elgar Publishing Limited
Glensanda House
Montpellier Parade
Cheltenham
Glos GL50 1UA
UK

Edward Elgar Publishing, Inc.
6 Market Street
Northampton
Massachusetts 01060
USA

1001735939

A catalogue record for this book
is available from the British Library

Library of Congress Cataloguing in Publication Data

Bommer, Rolf
    Economic integration and the environment: a political–economic
perspective / Rolf Bommer.
        (New horizons in environmental economics)
    Includes bibliographical references.
        1. International economic integration—environmental aspects.
    2. Commercial policy—Environmental aspects. 3. Environmental
policy. I. Title. II. Series.
    HF1418.5.B66 1998
    363.7—dc21   98–17087
                                                                    CIP

ISBN 1 85898 912 4

Printed and bound in Great Britain by
Biddles Ltd, Guildford and King's Lynn

Contents

Figures

Tables

Acknowledgements

This book was conceived at the research project 'Internationalization of the Economy' of the German Research Foundation at the University of Konstanz, Germany. I am most grateful to my adviser, Heinrich W. Ursprung, for his guidance from the beginning, the search for a subject and the scope, until the final completion. His advice, and his support in providing the funding, were invaluable for the successful realization of the study. I am also indebted to my second adviser, Albert Schweinberger. I profited substantially from his critical view on the political-economy paradigm and from his comments on aspects of international trade.

Furthermore, I benefited tremendously from help from the following individuals. Günther G. Schulze worked with me on NAFTA. Discussions with Arye Hillman in Silvaplana and in Israel proved to be key elements in locating the punchline of my argument. My colleagues Laszlo Goerke and Carsten Hefeker always had a minute to spare. My colleague Achim Körber, who has worked on 'ecoprotectionism', shared his ideas with me. Hans Peter Grüner helped when I was lost in the deep waters of game theory. Numerous colleagues at the Department of Economics and at the research project 'Internationalization of the Economy' contributed to shape my economic perspectives and to sharpen my arguments; with the post-lunch coffee hour they provided the work stimuli for the afternoon. Veena Jha of UNCTAD invited me to Geneva for a research fellowship and introduced the developing-country perspective on trade and the environment to me.

Lisa Green and Michele LaRoche kindly corrected my English. Nicole Burkhardt, Susanne Holder, Ulrike Sachs, Leo Schätz and Alexander Weißer eased my workload with excellent research assistance.

1 Introduction

The 1990s have witnessed an increasing concern about the environmental consequences of trade. Economic integration in many parts of the world raises fears that the environment could be severely damaged as trade expands production or alters the composition of production to a more polluting one.[1] For example, one of the most influential environmental organizations, Greenpeace, accuses the European Common Market of being a 'killer of the environment' (see Krägenow, 1996). Greenpeace warns that, for instance, the projected increase of truck traffic will cause environmental problems. The North American Free Trade Agreement (NAFTA) has come under heavy attack by environmentalists who fear that the United States will lower their environmental standards due to competition with Mexico, a country with lenient environmental standards. The attempts of the World Trade Organisation (WTO) to liberalize international trade are confronted with similar accusations.

Are these accusations justified? Does economic integration really cause a deterioration of the environment? Does free trade really induce a downward competition of environmental standards? The intention of this book is to analyze the links between trade and the environment. More specifically, it explains how the regulation of the environment is affected by economic integration. If countries integrate their economies by reducing trade barriers, what predictions can one make regarding changes in environmental policy? This question is considered from a political-economy perspective. Environmental regulation is determined in an institutional setting, in which self-interested policy makers interact with interest groups. Hence, environmental policy becomes endogenous.

This book on the *environmental policy effects of trade* builds on two different literatures. First, the literature on endogenous environmental policy provides the methodological framework. To a large extent, this literature investigates whether environmental regulation can be abused for the protectionist ambitions of producers. This issue became prominent under the

---

1   This study applies the term economic integration in a very broad sense. The term economic integration includes aspects of trade liberalization, regional trade agreements and political integration.

1

catchword 'eco-protectionism'. One example often reported, is the Tuna–dolphin case. The United States have limited the access of Mexican canned tuna to the US market allegedly for environmental reasons. Mexican fishing fleets are accused of killing considerably more dolphins when fishing tuna than US fishing fleets do. It is, however, suspected that the real underlying reason is the protection of the US fisheries from Mexican competition (see Vogel, 1995, Chapter 4). The second body of literature considered, addresses the question which I intend to deal with in this book: 'How does trade affect the environment?' The existing literature, however, views environmental regulation as given. This book encorporates the endogenous policy approach to environmental regulation into the analysis of the environmental effects of trade.

1.1 ENVIRONMENTAL POLICY AS A MEANS TO INFLUENCE TRADE

In the domain of trade and the environment the predominant question of the 1970s and 1980s has been about the effects of environmental policy on trade and competitiveness. Does environmental regulation adversely affect the competitiveness of producers? Does regulation drive producers to countries with more lenient regulation, to 'pollution havens'? More specifically, can environmental policies be abused for international trade reasons?

Analogous to the issue of strategic trade policy in the field of international economics, the question arises with regard to environmental policy making whether governments have incentives to relax or to tighten environmental standards to improve domestic firms' competitiveness against foreign rivals. The issue of lowering standards for strategic reasons became prominent under the label 'eco-dumping'. A further line of argument explores whether environmental regulation can be abused for the protectionist ambitions of producers. This issue is known as 'eco-protectionism'. Hence, the endogenous policy literature investigates how environmental regulation is utilized to facilitate the strategic ambitions of producers. These studies on eco-dumping and eco-protectionism are directly related to the literature on endogenous protection. Hillman (1989) and Rodrik (1995) review studies which explain the prevalence of trade protection even though most economists agree on the benefits of free trade.[2] With regard to capital

---

2   Here, we enter the field of 'second-best theory'. If there are market imperfections, for
    example, economies of scale, imperfect competition or externalities, the gains from free
    trade are less obvious than the standard textbook case suggests. Hence, there could always
    be an argument for restricting trade in a real-world setting. Therefore, most economists

controls, Schulze (1998) investigates the political-economy motives for restrictions on the free flow of capital, even though capital mobility is generally considered advantageous. The literature on endogenous environmental policy is linked to the literature on endogenous protection by adding a new instrument for controlling trade: environmental policy.

Environmental policy is endogenously determined for political-economic reasons. Policy makers, voters and bureaucrats are portrayed as rational and self-interested agents, just as in neoclassical economic theory consumers and producers are taken to be rational and self-interested. Environmental regulation is determined by the interaction of these self-interested agents. Endogenous policy theory investigates why certain policies *are selected*. This objective contrasts with classical environmental economics, which provides policy recommendations on how environmental policy *should be selected*. Endogenous policy analysis investigates why so few environmental regulations satisfy the normative prescriptions of environmental economists: we observe neither market-based environmental instruments in abundance, nor efficient levels of regulation.

Not all political agents are decisive for the political outcome. This book is concerned mostly with the interaction of politicians, producers and environmentalists in the determination of environmental policy in a representative democracy. Voters are not considered since they are perceived as being rationally ignorant. They choose to remain uninformed when undertaking a simple cost–benefit comparison: the costs of obtaining political information are high where their benefits (as individuals among millions of others) are low. Rationally ignorant voters allow politicians to gain discretionary power which they can use to follow their own objectives, for example, by maximizing political support or their re-election probabilities. Producers may lobby for low environmental standards which regulate production activities (eco-dumping). Moreover, producers may gain from tight product standards since product standards may be helpful to obtain a competitive advantage against foreign producers in a 'raising rivals' cost' manner. In contrast to producers, environmentalists are motivated by their interest for a cleaner environment. However, the environmentalists may side with the demands of producers for inefficient environmental regulations since inefficient regulation may be the only way to obtain environmental protection at all. In this respect, environmentalists may become the 'potential bedfellows of interests that have less pure objectives in influencing trade policy than the environmentalists impute to themselves' (Hillman and Ursprung, 1994).

follow the reasoning of Krugman, who states that the free-trade paradigm serves as a 'good rule of thumb' (see Krugman, 1987).

1.2   ECONOMIC INTEGRATION AND THE ENVIRONMENT: TWO DIFFERENT POSITIONS

Above, it is suggested that environmental policy is determined by the interaction of self-interested politicians, environmentalists and producers. Hence, in this book environmental policy is viewed as being endogenous. However, the literature which explores the environmental effects of economic integration views environmental policy as given. The major controversy, raised by this literature, is presented in this section before the endogenous approach to economic integration and the environment is introduced.

On the one hand, proponents of free trade state that the environment of countries participating in free-trade agreements may improve if environmental policies are in place. In this regard, remarks by the OECD are typical (OECD, 1995, p. 11):

> As a rule, the liberalisation of trade improves the efficient allocation of resources, promotes economic growth and increases general welfare. It can promote the diffusion of environmentally-beneficial goods and services. It also provides incentives to improve environmental standards and regulations and facilitates the transfer of environmentally sound technologies. Moreover, trade liberalisation contributes to developing environmental management capacity in developing countries. These beneficial effects will, however, depend upon the extent to which countries implement environmental policies conducive to sustainable development ...

On the other hand, trade critics claim that free trade and liberalized capital movements cause a deterioration in the environment. One of the leading environmentalist critics of free trade, Herman Daly (1994), warns that free trade overburdens the limited carrying capacities of the earth. This argument is based on the belief that environmental and natural resources are not readily substitutable by human capital and technology. Hence, if free trade expands output, the environment would necessarily deteriorate. Furthermore, many trade critics believe, even if the internalization of environmental externalities is possible, that free trade inhibits the internalization of environmental problems as countries engage in a downward competition of standards (eco-dumping). They fear that producers will relocate their firms to low-standard pollution havens. In this regard, Daly and Goodland (1994, pp. 77–8) claim that international trade will increase competition between countries whereby low-standard countries impose pressure on other countries to relax their standards for competitiveness reasons:[3]

> A country that internalizes environmental costs into its prices will be at a disadvantage, at least in the short run, in unregulated trade with a country that does not internalize environmental costs. Therefore, national protection of a basic policy of internalization of environmental costs constitutes a clear justification for tariffs on imports from a country which does not internalize its environmental costs. This is not protectionism in the usual sense of protecting an inefficient industry, but rather the protection of an efficient national policy of internalization of environmental costs.

The two groups, free-traders versus environmentalists, provide different insights on the interlinkages between trade and the environment. Both approach the issue one-sidedly. Critics of free trade focus only on the negative aspects of free trade by emphasizing the dangers of free trade, while neglecting its economic and environmental opportunities. For instance, they claim that growth causes more pollution and that trade causes a deterioration in the environment by creating opportunities for the export of hazardous waste. They also claim that free trade contributes to the relocation of industries to pollution havens, which results in the specialization of low-standard countries in the production of pollution-intensive goods. On the other hand, the proponents of free trade focus only on efficiency and welfare improvements from trade liberalization. They argue that rising output, and hence rising income, increases the demand for environmental goods. Further, trade causes opportunities for the diffusion of 'clean' goods. Finally, by pointing to the experience from inward-oriented development policies in socialist countries, where environmental deterioration took place on a large scale, they claim that autarky can be no solution at all. For example, the focus on inefficient heavy industries and centrally planned agriculture in China has caused considerable environmental deterioration in the years prior to reform (see Smil, 1984).

1.3 A NEW APPROACH TO THE DEBATE ON ECONOMIC INTEGRATION AND THE ENVIRONMENT

This study draws on both bodies of literature presented above to investigate an issue which is neglected in the debate on trade and the environment: the

---

3 Other studies arguing for limits to free trade for environmental reasons include Shrybman (1990), Young (1994) and Røpke (1994).

influence of economic integration on environmental policy making. First, from a methodological point of view, this study is closely linked to the endogenous policy literature which examines how environmental policy can be abused for pressure group demands with respect to international trade. This link is explored in Section 2. Second, the literature on the environmental effects of trade is explored in Section 3. But in contrast to this literature, the determination of environmental policy is addressed explicitly (Figure 1.1).

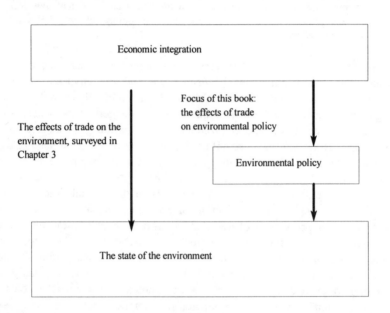

Figure 1.1: The effects of economic integration on the environment

This study explains how environmental policy is changed by trade liberalization, instead of taking environmental policy as given. Environmental policy is endogenous to economic integration since integration affects the stakes of the interest groups, which, in turn, influence environmental policy. With the abolition of trade protection, import-competing sectors, confronted with foreign competition, may suffer heavy losses and may lobby for more lenient environmental standards. Depending on whether groups are losing or gaining from free trade, they demand compensating adjustments or they may relax their lobbying.

There are links between trade policies and environmental policies and vice versa. One approach of endogenous policy analysis addresses the determination of trade policies, but views environmental policy as given. This approach is chosen by Hillman and Ursprung (1994), who examine how the appearance of environmentalists affects the political equilibrium of trade protection. The focus of this book is a different one. While the determination of environmental policy is investigated, trade policy is viewed as given. This study is concerned with how environmental policy is changed in the process of economic integration.[4] The dichotomous treatment, exogenous trade policies and endogenous environmental policies, is justified by the temporal dimension of policy formation. Trade agreements, once in place, cannot easily be abrogated unilaterally, but environmental policies can be changed unilaterally. After economic integration is implemented, it takes time until its effects materialize. Economic integration has distributional consequences and will cause opposition which the government must appease, possibly with the help of environmental policy. The response of environmental policy with respect to a change in trade policy is confirmed by the example of negotiations on the NAFTA trade agreement. The environmental parts of the agreement were added after economic integration principles had been agreed upon (see Chapter 4).

Up to now, the effects of trade on environmental regulation were hardly explored. Therefore, even though this book addresses most of the topical issues, some limits remain. For the most part, the environmental issues considered are limited to domestic pollution problems. However, an extension regarding aspects of transboundary pollution spillovers is provided in Chapter 5. Moreover, aspects of trade diversion and trade creation, due to trade integration, are not explored. Furthermore, the topical discussion on the justification of trade measures for environmental purposes is skipped since this study emphasizes positive issues.[5] Finally, this study is largely limited to a theoretical analysis. Only Section 4.3 investigates empirically the environmental consequences of NAFTA in the United States.

---

4 Of course, trade policy is another tool of political support-maximizing governments. For example, Hillman and Moser (1996) have shown that the political-economic rationale for free trade agreements is the mutual exchange of market access.

5 Standard analysis on trade and the environment concludes that environmental problems should be solved at their source. Therefore, trade policies should not be used for environmental reasons. However, when pollution is transboundary or even global, recommendations are less clear-cut. In international environmental agreements, for example, the Montreal Protocol and the Convention on International Trade and Endangered Species (CITES), trade measures are introduced to ensure compliance of participating and non-participating countries. For more on this issue, see Esty (1994a), GATT (1993b), Siebert (1998), Subramanian (1992), and Kirchgässner and Mohr (1996).

1.4 THE STRUCTURE OF THE BOOK

This book consists of seven chapters. The introductory Chapters 2 and 3 review the literatures on which this study is based. Chapter 2 reviews the literature on the trade effects of environmental regulation, the environment–trade link. It is shown that environmental regulation may be able to affect trade and investment patterns, and, hence, the competitiveness of industries. Therefore, environmental policy can be abused by policy makers as a means of improving the competitiveness of domestic producers by reducing their cost through low regulation (eco-dumping), or by restraining market access to foreign competitors (eco-protectionism). The ability to influence output and profits using environmental regulation is the basis of an endogenous environmental-policy perspective which is reviewed in Chapter 2 as well. This endogenous perspective is one of the two pillars of this study.

The study's second pillar, the literature on the environmental effects of trade, is introduced in Chapter 3. While the literature considers the environmental effects caused by a change in scale and composition in the economy as a result of free trade, this book investigates the *environmental effects* of trade by applying the *endogenous environmental-policy* perspective reviewed in Chapter 2. Therefore, the focus is on the *environmental-policy effects* of trade. Each of the Chapters 4, 5 and 6 addresses the same crucial question – the impact of free trade on environmental policy – but considers very different set-ups: perfect competition, imperfect competition and, finally, asymmetric information.

Chapter 4 addresses the evidence on NAFTA, which predicts an increase of pollution-intensive production in the US due to NAFTA and, hence, a deteriorating US environment. This result is based on studies reviewed in Chapter 3, taking environmental regulation as given. Chapter 4 argues, relying on a model of international trade with perfect competition, that the endogenous reaction of environmental policy leads to tighter standards in the US, a fact which mitigates the predicted environmental harm of free trade.

Chapter 5 applies an environmental-policy adaptation of international trade models of imperfect competition to analyze the impact of economic integration on the environment. These models, reviewed in Chapter 2, find that eco-dumping, the downward competition of environmental standards to inefficient low levels, is possible. By relying on such eco-dumping approaches, this chapter explores the effects of economic integration with particular reference to European integration. It is shown that downward competition of standards can be overcome by integration-induced cooperation.

Chapter 6, again, considers the concern that economic integration induces a downward competition of standards. In a set-up of imperfect competition and asymmetric information, firms are no longer passive actors, but are able to shift their production facilities to pollution havens to escape tight regulation at home. Furthermore, producers relocate their production facilities to influence environmental policy making. They relocate their facilities to pressure the domestic government into lowering domestic pollution standards. This is called the pollution-haven debate. Considering a model of imperfect competition and asymmetric information, the consequences of free trade on the relocation decisions of producers are investigated. It is shown that integration can increase the probability of strategic relocation because the costs of relocation fall. Consequently, policy makers relax environmental regulation not because environmental regulation has real adverse effects on output, but only because the producer relocates with the intention of deceiving the policy maker about his or her ability to cope with tighter regulation.

Chapter 7 provides conclusions and discusses policy recommendations. One major contribution of this book is that some simple 'truths' regarding the environmental effects of free trade are questioned. If the environment deteriorates because of free trade – which is not certain at all – then there are endogenous policy reactions which can induce tighter environmental regulation and, thereby, mitigate or prevent environmental harm. Such a deeper understanding may contribute to a better acceptance of free trade in the future.

2 Trade and the Environment: An Overview

This chapter motivates the discussion about the interface of trade and the environment from a political-economic point of view.[1] There are two aspects to be highlighted:

- Does domestic environmental regulation jeopardize the trade opportunities of domestic producers?
- Do stringent environmental policies drive producers to pollution havens?

If environmental policies have the power to influence trade patterns and to create pollution havens, does this induce a 'rat race', which is driving down environmental standards to inefficiently low levels? This question became prominent when environmental regulation became more restrictive in the mid-1970s and, consequently, fears regarding adverse effects on international competitiveness have risen as well.[2]

Section 2.1 discusses the role of the environment within the framework of the theory of international trade. Section 2.2 gives an overview of the theoretical and empirical studies on the interface of environment and trade; the emphasis is on the debate on competitiveness and the environment. Finally, Section 2.3 reviews studies which apply an endogenous policy perspective with regard to the environment and its links to trade.

---

1   The expanding literature on trade and the environment is surveyed by Ulph (1996b), Dean (1992), Rauscher (1996) and Schulze and Ursprung (1997). Valuable volumes in this field are Low (1992a) and Anderson and Blackhurst (1992).
2   For example, the total cost of pollution control in the US rose from 1.74 percent of GNP in 1972 to 2.61 percent of GNP in 1982 (Jaffe et al., 1995). Since the early 1990s, another push of environmental concern, to a significant degree caused by 'new' environmental problems with global consequences, that is, global warming, ozone depletion and the loss of biodiversity, raises regulatory density even further.

2.1 THE ENVIRONMENT AND THE CONCEPT OF COMPARATIVE ADVANTAGE

Standard trade theory argues that countries maximize their welfare if each country specializes in the production of goods in which it has a comparative advantage.[3] Each country exports the goods which it can produce *relatively* cheaper than other countries. More specifically, in the standard 2×2×2 Heckscher–Ohlin model with identical technologies, the country endowed with a factor of production relatively abundantly, produces the good which needs this factor of production relatively intensively. The incorporation of the environment into trade modeling is straightforward: the environment is introduced as a production factor, an approach which is standard in environmental economics.[4] The endowment with the factor environment[5] determines comparative advantage; the country which is endowed relatively abundantly with 'environment' gains a comparative advantage in the production of environment-intensive goods and, therefore, specializes in the production of environment-intensive goods.

Siebert (1995) suggests three factors which determine the endowment with the factor environment and, closely related, the politics governing the use of the environment. First, the 'environmental endowment' depends on the ability of natural systems to assimilate pollutants.[6] Second, the demand for the environment as a medium of discharging wastes by producers and consumers determines assimilative capacities. Third, the competing use of the environment as a consumption good determines the opportunity costs of discharging wastes. According to a country's endowment in environment, trade induces the country's specialization either in the production of environment-intensive goods or in goods requiring the environment to a lesser extent. If the endowment with 'environment' is chosen properly, that is, the right environmental policy is chosen, efficiency gains from trade are guaranteed. The optimality criterion for the right environmental policy requires that the marginal benefits of using the environment as an input of production or as a receptacle of wastes have to equal the marginal damage of

3 Besides this necessary condition for the gains from trade, some sufficient conditions are required: perfect competition in goods and factor markets and constant returns to scale.
4 For an overview on environmental economics and, more specifically, on the various attempts of modeling the environment as a production factor, see Cropper and Oates (1992).
5 If not indicated otherwise, the terms environment, pollution and emissions are used synonymously.
6 The natural environment in the Persian Gulf, for instance, has a much higher ability to cope with oil spills than arctic environments. For example, the Persian Gulf recovered relatively easily from huge amounts of oil released in consequence of the Gulf war when compared to the difficult recovery for a comparably small oil spill in the Prince William Sound in Alaska.

pollution. Depending on the specialization pattern, trade may well induce increased pollution in certain countries which specialize in environmental-intensive goods; but if the environment is regulated properly, the efficiency gains of trade are not impaired.

Since the optimality criterion for environmental policy is often not satisfied, efficiency gains from free trade are no longer trivial; environmental deterioration may offset the efficiency gains from trade. Nevertheless, there is a consensus among economists that the uncertainty with respect to the gains from trade for environmental reasons should not require trade restrictions to preserve the environment.[7] Applying trade policies as an environmental remedy has only very indirect and limited effects. From a normative point of view, trade policy is only a second-, third-, or *x*-best measure for solving environment problems. The first-best solution requires appropriate environmental policies at the source of the environmental problem.

This section has provided recommendations for how environmental policies *should* be chosen. This is the normative reference point for the positive analysis undertaken in this study. In the following section, the question of how environmental policies *are* chosen, is investigated.

2.2 ENVIRONMENT AND TRADE MODELING

This section gives an overview of the theoretical and empirical studies on environment and trade, where the particular emphasis is on positive and distributive issues to motivate the political-economy approach chosen in this book. Two types of models which are relevant for a political-economy investigation are reviewed.

First, the distributional impact of environmental regulation is of importance because gainers or losers from environmental regulations will attempt to influence environmental policy making. These studies are based on Heckscher–Ohlin-type or specific-factor-type models of perfect competition, where the focus is on the effects of policies on factor returns and on the terms of trade. Second, models with imperfect competition, based on the 'new trade theory', are introduced. These models, which consider the opportunities of strategic behavior for governments and producers, investigate whether fears regarding a 'downward' competition of standards are justified. In both approaches, environmental policy becomes a substitute for trade policy.

---

7   See Schweinberger (1997) for necessary and sufficient conditions under which the gains from trade can still be guaranteed, even if environmental externalities are not completely internalized.

Besides the issue of perfect versus imperfect competition, there is a second issue at stake. The governments' choice of environmental regulation depends on whether trade is only in goods, keeping production factors internationally immobile, or whether the mobility of factors is considered explicitly. Table 2.1 distinguishes the studies reviewed with respect to these two issues.

Table 2.1: A survey of the studies on trade and the environment

	Perfect competition	**Imperfect competition**
Trade in goods	Pethig (1975), Yohe (1979), Forster (1981), McGuire (1982), Krutilla (1991), Rauscher (1991a), Rauscher (1994), Merryfield (1988)	Barrett (1994), Conrad (1996a, b), Ulph (1992), Ulph (1996a)
Factor (capital) movements	Siebert et al. (1980), Long and Siebert (1991), Oates and Schwab (1988), Rauscher (1991b)	Markusen et al. (1993), Markusen et al. (1995), Pflüger (1996), Motta and Thisse (1994)

2.2.1   Environmental Regulation when Factors are Immobile

Competitive markets

Models with competitive markets focus on the specialization pattern of countries when the factor environment is considered. The concern is on inter-industry trade, that is, what are the causes of specialization in pollution-intensive goods or in clean goods. Models of imperfectly competitive markets, which open up the issue of intra-industry trade, are discussed below. In an early paper, Pethig (1975) considers the welfare consequences of trade if no environmental policy is in place. He extends a standard 2×2×2 Heckscher–Ohlin model of international trade with the environment as a factor of production. Country 1 specializes in the pollution-intensive good D and country 2 in the clean good C. Even though pollution from production is completely local, he shows that pollution can be indirectly exported: by restricting trade, country 1 is able to shift pollution to country 2 since production in country 1 declines while production expands in country 2. Since welfare gains from trade are offset by environmental losses, country 1 has an incentive to restrict trade according to 'pollute thy neighbor via trade', whereas country 2 wishes to expand trade.

A first step in a political-economic investigation is the analysis of the distributional implications of environmental policies. The effects of environmental regulation on factor returns are introduced by Yohe (1979), who considers a two-good model of a small open economy with given prices and the three factors capital, labor and environment. The environment serves as an input in producing the pollution-intensive good D. The pollution standard reduces the return of the factor, which is used relatively intensively in good D, whereas the pollution standard raises the return of the factor, used relatively intensively in the clean good. In a similar model with pollution taxes, McGuire (1982) comes to the same conclusions.

Forster (1981) extends Yohe's analysis by considering a Ricardo–Viner setting, as introduced by Jones (1971) with two sectors D and C and the two factors labor and environment. Labor is mobile between sectors, whereas environment is sector-specific. Regulation restricting the use of the environment in the production sector D reduces labor productivity in this sector. Hence, labor moves sector C. The wage rate in the economy falls since less of the factor environment is available. An extended version of a Ricardo–Viner model with the factors environment, labor and sector-specific capital serves in Chapter 4 as the distributional basis for a political-economic analysis of trade liberalization and the environment.

In such a small country, by definition, not only world market prices, but all other foreign variables, are given. This is the small-open-economy assumption. Environmental policies can only influence the distribution inside the country and, therefore, cannot explain conflicts between countries regarding their trade and environmental policies. A step in this direction is done by replacing the small-open-economy assumption by considering a large country. A large country can influence foreign variables and, therefore, the issue of eco-dumping can be explored. This literature follows the optimal-tariff argument (Johnson, 1953/4). In a two-sector model, Krutilla (1991) shows how environmental policy can be utilized to improve the terms of trade of a large trading country. If production of the export good causes environmental externalities, a restrictive environmental policy increases the cost of production and, consequently, the price of the good. Since the large country is able to influence world-market prices, environmental regulation causes an improvement in the terms of trade. The result is the opposite from eco-dumping: standards will be higher than efficient if the export good is pollution intensive. Conversely, if the production of the import good causes the environmental damage, then restrictive environmental regulation increases the price of the import good and, hence, induces a fall in the terms of trade. Therefore, the country undertakes eco-dumping to improve its terms of trade if the import good is 'dirty'.[8] In a 2×2×2 model with a pollution tax and the factors of production capital and environment, Rauscher (1991a) arrives at conclusions similar to Krutilla's: 'If a country is an exporter (importer) of pollution-intensive goods, the optimal tax rate is higher (lower) than the tax rate that internalizes social cost'.

In a similar model with traded and non-traded goods, Rauscher (1994) explores the possibilities for eco-dumping. Two factors of production, capital and environment, are inputs in the non-traded-good sector 1 and in the traded-good sector 2; good 3 is only imported. A production externality causes local pollution. Relaxing environmental regulation in the traded-good sector 2 has the same result as found by Rauscher (1991a) and Krutilla (1991): output of good 2 increases, depresses the price of good 2 and reduces the terms of trade. The effect on the non-traded sector 1 is not clear-cut: output of good 1 increases since capital is attracted away from sector 2. Output of sector 2 falls with the consequence of a rising price and improving terms of trade. On the other hand, increasing output in sector 1 decreases the price of good 1 and shifts capital into the traded-goods sector 2, where it causes a decline in the terms of trade.

Even though effects are not clear-cut, the terms-of-trade literature reveals that cases exist where – contrary to the predictions of the eco-dumping argument – non-export sectors obtain relief from environmental regulation, whereas exporters have to cope with particularly strict standards. However, there are caveats in the studies presented above. Terms-of-trade results change if capital mobility and pollution spillovers are considered. In a two-country model with mobile capital, Merryfield (1988) assumes that each country has one sector of production, producing different goods in each country. The factor environment increases the productivity of capital, but pollutes both countries. A pollution tax in one country reduces domestic emissions, but makes capital less productive. Capital moves abroad, where rising output increases foreign pollution to the home country via transboundary spillovers. Via international capital mobility, a domestic environmental tax has sizable repercussion effects, which limit not only the tax's environmental benefits, but also the aspired terms-of-trade effects.

The terms-of-trade approach has a further shortcoming. It investigates only the behavior of one country and neglects possible retaliation actions of other countries affected by strategic environmental regulation. The following

8   These results hold only if no other policies, such as import or export taxes, are in place. Krutilla (1991) extends the analysis to consumption externalities. He discovers that if the export good causes consumption externalities, the negative terms-of-trade effect from strict environmental regulation offsets the positive effect of a cleaner environment. Consumption regulation of the polluting good increases the country's initial level of excess supply which induces a downward pressure of the world price, with the consequence being a decrease in terms of trade.

subsection presents approaches which overcome this problem by considering non-cooperative behavior of more than one country regarding the choice of environmental policy.

Strategic environmental regulation in non-competitive markets

In the 1980s, the 'new trade theory' emerged, examining the implications of trade polices in non-competitive markets.[9] The new trade theory opened up the possibilities of analyzing environmental regulation with regard to intra-industry trade. In contrast to the approaches presented above, producers in non-competitive markets are able to earn profits. Governments choose environmental polices to raise the profits of 'their' producers. Although governments are still modeled as social welfare maximizers – consumer surplus and environmental amenities – the modeling of the strategic interaction of governments and producers bears similarities to the political-economic analysis undertaken below. A seminal paper on the new trade theory is from Brander and Spencer (1985), who analyze a setting of two firms, a foreign and a domestic one, which compete in quantities on a third, foreign market. Brander and Spencer show in their model that a firm increases production if the home government increases R&D and export subsidies. Subsidies move the industry equilibrium to the Stackelberg point. The literature on trade and the environment applies the new trade theory for its own purpose: instead of R&D and export subsidies, it investigates the effects of environmental policy on the strategic interaction of producers.

In the tradition of the new trade theory, Barrett (1994) considers a stage game involving two governments and their respective producers, who sell their output on a third market. In the first stage of the game, the governments set environmental standards, and in the second stage, the respective producers decide on production. Unlike most of the studies relying on the analysis of competitive markets, in which the environment is modeled as a factor of production, the environment is introduced only implicitly by a costly production standard. The governments face a trade-off between maximizing producer profits and minimizing damage from production-related emissions. Barrett's results depend on the type of competition and on the number of firms. If the domestic and the foreign firms are the sole producers in their countries, acting in quantity competition (Cournot–Nash), each government sets the environmental standard by taking the standard of the other government as given. The governments' motivation is rent shifting for the benefit of their domestic producers. In the policy equilibrium, both governments set standards which are *below* the efficient standard.[10] This is an

9   See Helpman and Krugman (1989), for instance.
10 The efficient standard is characterized by the equalization of the marginal cost of standard setting and the marginal damage of pollution.

eco-dumping argument: by allowing more pollution, each government increases output and profits of the domestic producer. If both governments act strategically, they are worse off compared to a cooperative setting of environmental standards. They are caught in a prisoner's dilemma, whereby the competition forces their standards *below* efficient levels.

However, this result does not hold for other market structures and other types of producer competition. Barrett (1994) shows that if the foreign industry is competitive and only the domestic industry is oligopolistic, the domestic government may possibly set a standard which is *above* the efficient standard. Under these circumstances, a high standard may improve profits by the reduction of the oligopolists' output. Furthermore, a different type of competition between oligopolists reverses the results. If duopolists are involved in Bertrand price competition, the equilibrium standard is *above* the efficient standard. A strong emission standard raises marginal costs but justifies a price rise of the producers as well. Therefore, unlike in the Cournot case, the producers welcome a stricter standard if profits rise. The strategic-environmental-policy modeling is also sensitive to a change in other assumptions. Conrad (1996a and 1996b) shows that results may well reverse when using a variant of Barrett's model which allows for consumption in the producers' countries. With regard to quantity competition of duopolists, Conrad (1996a) finds that the emission tax rate may be *above* the optimal level. For Bertrand competition, Conrad (1996b) shows that the emission tax rate may be *below* the optimal level.[11]

The impact of transboundary pollution on the eco-dumping results of the previous studies is explored by Kennedy (1994). When considering a model of *n* firms in each of two countries, the firms produce one homogenous good and compete in quantities. A pollution tax, applied to control the domestic pollution effects of production, has two effects. First, a rent-capture effect lowers equilibrium pollution taxes since each country seeks to improve its producers' competitiveness by capturing foreign rents through exports. A pollution-shifting effect raises the pollution tax in the manner of 'pollute thy neighbor via trade'. As shown in some of the models reviewed above, he finds that the pollution tax is lower than the efficient level; the rent-capture effect dominates the pollution-shifting effect. If pollution is transboundary, production causes pollution externalities in the other country, thereby

---

11   The choice of the instrument of protection is considered by Ulph (1992), who presents a three-stage model in which governments choose environmental policies in the first stage and firms choose capital stock and output level at the second and third stages. He finds that strategically acting governments set pollution standards rather than pollution taxes because standards allow firms to commit to reduced output. This commitment increases their profits.

reinforcing the rent-capture effect and relaxing pollution regulation even further.[12]

These models on the strategic use of environmental policy provide a foundation for the investigation of the impact of European integration on the environment, undertaken in Chapter 5. Both results found in the literature, the downward competition of standards, obtained by Barrett (1994) under certain assumptions, and the reinforcement of downward competition if transboundary externalities are considered (see Kennedy, 1994), are obtained in Chapter 5 for the case of non-cooperating countries as well. However, it is shown that the institutional set-up of the European Union facilitates the cooperation of policy makers and, therefore, avoids the downward competition of standards.

2.2.2 Environmental Regulation and Capital Mobility

The previous subsection has considered the effects of environmental regulation on trade in goods, in which capital was assumed to be mobile only between sectors within the economy. Now, we ask another question. What is the impact of environmental regulation on the international location of production? In this regard, fears are described with the label 'pollution-haven hypothesis': pollution-intensive industries are expected to relocate to countries with lax environmental regulations. Again, as undertaken in the previous subsection, two types of models are reviewed. First, models with perfect competition are presented, before approaches using a non-competitive market structure are reviewed.

In models with competitive markets and capital mobility (see, for example, Long and Siebert, 1991; Oates and Schwab, 1988), the consequences of environmental policy are obvious: strict environmental regulation reduces the profitability of capital; hence, capital is relocated abroad. Long and Siebert (1991) developed a model with two countries, the two factors labor and capital, and one sector of production. The use of capital causes pollution and, hence, is regulated with a pollution tax. The pollution tax decreases the return of capital, with the consequence that capital moves to the foreign country until the rental rates of capital in both countries equalize.[13] The outflow of

---

12 Models with strategically acting producers and governments can be extended by allowing for R&D decisions of producers. Ulph (1996a) presents a model where R&D investment reduces production cost and where lenient environmental regulation increases the profitability of R&D investment. A lenient standard increases the incentive of producers to invest strategically in R&D to improve their competitive position against foreign rivals. The beneficial effects on competitiveness increase the government's incentive to choose a lenient environmental standard. However, Ulph (1994) shows that results may alter if R&D investments reduce emissions rather than production costs.

13 See Section 3.4 on the analysis of the effects of capital-market liberalization on the environment in a similar two-country set-up, undertaken by Rauscher (1991b).

capital makes capital more scarce in the home country, resulting in a decline of the domestic wage rate and in an increase of the foreign wage rate since capital is more abundant in the foreign country. If there are no further externalities, Long and Siebert find that the emission tax is chosen according to the cost of marginal damage. The outcome is efficient.

When considering a model of *n* countries, one non-traded good, the mobile factor capital and immobile labor and environment, Oates and Schwab (1988) draw the same conclusions. However, the result changes if, besides the environmental externality, a second distortion, a tax on capital, is introduced. Oates and Schwab show in a two-country setting that the marginal benefits of the pollution tax exceed the cost of improving the environment: environmental regulation is inefficiently low. The fiscal effect from environmental regulation, the loss in capital tax, drives a wedge in the benefits and costs of regulation. Both countries set lower than optimal environmental regulation because they do not take the positive effect of their regulations on the foreign country, the benefits from the relocation of capital, into account.

Results differ considerably in models of imperfect competition. Markusen et al. (1995) consider the case of a single firm with increasing returns to scale at the plant level, serving imperfect competitive markets in two countries. In the first stage of the game, both countries influence the investment decision by an environmental tax. In a second stage, the firm decides whether to produce in only one or both countries. Markusen et al. distinguish two cases with discrete solutions: if environmental damage from production is large, both countries drive the firm with a high pollution standard off the market. This is known as the not-in-my-backyard (NIMBY) scenario. If environmental damage is small, both countries are in a rat race, that is, driving down standards with the intention of attracting the investor. Pflüger (1996) comes to similar conclusions by applying a general-equilibrium model of monopolistic competition. In his set-up, there are two countries which produce differentiated manufactured goods with increasing returns to scale and a homogeneous good with constant returns to scale. Firms use capital, labor and the environment, which is regulated by an emission tax. A unilateral rise of one country's emission tax has three effects on the other country. First, capital becomes more profitable with the consequence that firms relocate. Second, the tax income increases with increasing tax base, and, third, pollution rises as production expands. If disutility from pollution is small, countries are caught up in a rat race, that is driving down standards. If disutility from pollution is large, countries drive up emission taxes; the consequence is a NIMBY scenario.

In a similar two-country model on location choice by Markusen et al. (1993), the market structure becomes endogenous. In the first stage of the game, the governments regulate pollution which is caused by production. Each of the two producers, located in one of the two countries, decides in a second stage whether to invest at home and serve foreign demand by exports, or whether to build a plant in the other country. The variable costs of producing at home are larger than abroad, but a possible investment abroad causes higher fixed costs. They find that only small differences in the pollution regulation between both countries cause producers to locate abroad. A variant of this model by Motta and Thisse (1994) assumes that the firms are already established at home. Therefore, the firms' set-up costs are already sunk, from which it follows that relocation is less attractive. If sunk costs are large, Motta and Thisse conclude that relocation is not a likely outcome of stricter environmental regulation. However, they emphasize that the result is driven by quantity competition of producers and expect results to reverse if producers compete in prices. Chapter 6 of this study presents a different approach regarding location decisions and the environment: producers may strategically shift capital abroad to pressure the government into not tightening environmental regulation.

The theoretical studies on the impact of environmental regulation on trade patterns and on location decisions do not come to systematic conclusions. Studies building upon the small-open-economy framework find that environmental polices decrease the rental rate of factors which are used relatively intensively in pollution-intensive goods. Consequently, if factors are mobile only domestically, strict environmental regulation induces sectoral changes within the economy; the sector producing the pollution-intensive good shrinks at the expense of the clean sector of production. If countries with competitive markets are large, environmental policy may be used equivalently to an optimal tariff in trade policy. A country with pollution-intensive export production will choose a strict standard to improve its terms of trade. However, the result reverses if the pollution-intensive sector is import competing: eco-dumping will take place since a low standard improves the terms of trade. In the case of imperfect competition, the results depend on the type of competition. If producers compete in quantities, governments drive down their standards to inefficiently low levels. If competition is in prices, standards will turn out to be inefficiently strict. Research on location decisions under imperfect competition comes to similarly unclear results. Either governments drive up their standards to push producers out of the country (the NIMBY scenario) or governments reduce their standards to inefficiently low levels to attract investment. In the next subsection, the empirical evidence is reviewed.

2.2.3 The Empirical Evidence[14]

To analyze the impact of environmental regulation on trade and investment, the empirical literature estimates the pollution content of trade. It is investigated whether an increase in the strictness of a country's environmental regulation causes the relative pollution content of exports to imports to decline. If the relative pollution content declines, environmental policy may be responsible for a decline of competitiveness of dirty (export) production. Most studies measure the pollution content of trade by the use of pollution abatement and control expenditures (PACE), which measure the cost of regulation in each sector of production. PACE capture the producer's cost burden of pollution regulation. A second measure of pollution intensity, toxic release data, directly measures emissions for estimating the pollution intensity of production. [15]

Environmental policy and trade patterns
Walter (1973) applied an input–output analysis to estimate PACE per unit of output in 83 American manufacturing and service industries. For the years between 1968 and 1970 he obtained a pollution-cost ratio of imports to exports of 0.87, whereby the PACE share of exports was 1.75 percent and the PACE share for imports only 1.52 percent.[16] The pollution-cost ratio, he found, suggests that the US specialized in comparatively dirty production.[17] Robison (1988) extended the study by Walter (1973) for the years between 1973 and 1982, a period of rapidly rising environmental regulation. He estimated that pollution cost became higher for imports than for exports. The ratio of PACE for imports to exports increased from 1.15 to 1.39. He concludes that the US specialized in comparatively clean production and, hence, may have experienced a decline in competitiveness of dirty US industries.

Based on PACE data, Tobey (1990) selected industries with a PACE share higher than 1.85 percent as pollution-intensive and grouped them into the five sectors: mining, paper, chemicals, steel and nonferrous metals. In a second step, Tobey used an index measuring the stringency of pollution-control measures in many countries for the five pollution-intensive sectors.

---

14 For other surveys, see Dean (1992) and Jaffe et al. (1995).
15 See Appendix 2A for details and limitations of PACE and toxic release.
16 Other estimates for PACE are presented by Robison (1985) and Low (1992b). Robison estimates an industry average of 3 percent of turnover, whereas electricity generation accounts for a PACE share of 5.4 percent. Without using input–output analysis, Low (1992b) finds a PACE share of only 0.54 percent of turnover for 1988 US manufacturing. Cement is the dirtiest industry with a PACE share of 3 percent.
17 With regard to the Heckscher–Ohlin theorem, one could argue that the US is well endowed with the production factor environment.

He regressed net exports, the dependent variable, on regulation stringency and other non-environmental variables. He found that environmental stringency was in no case a significant determinant of net exports. In a study of 78 industries, Kalt (1988) regressed changes in net exports on PACE and other variables for the years between 1967 and 1977. Like Tobey (1990), he was not able to find a significant relationship between compliance cost and net exports for the complete sample. However, restricting the sample to manufacturing industries, he obtained a significant negative relationship between compliance costs and net exports.

Low and Yeats (1992) examined the trade pattern of the US and South-East Asian countries between 1965 and 1988. According to their results, the share of world trade in dirty products declined from 19 percent to 16 percent. The share of dirty US exports declined particularly drastically from 21 percent to 14 percent. On the other hand, the share of dirty South-East Asian exports increased from 3.4 percent to 8.4 percent. However, not only the pollution intensity of less-developed-country exports increased; according to Lucas et al. (1992), production in LDCs was characterized by high growth rates of pollution-intensive sectors in the years between 1960 and 1988.

Environmental policy and location choice
Several studies searched for evidence regarding the pollution-haven hypothesis: pollution-intensive industries are suspected of relocating to countries with lax environmental regulation, in particular LDCs. These studies found no significant link between the stringency of environmental regulation and location decisions.[18] Leonard (1988) examined foreign investment of multinational corporations. He found that compliance costs with environmental regulations are, as opposed to other factors of location, of only marginal significance. Similar conclusions are drawn by Bartik (1988), who investigated location decisions of Fortune-500 companies inside the US. McConnell and Schwab (1990) found no significant effects of environmental regulation on location decisions in the motor vehicle industry by examining 50 new plant openings between 1973 and 1982.

Despite the fact that there is no systematic evidence for the pollution-haven hypothesis, several studies report specific industries in which environmental variables led to relocation. Gray and Walter (1983) observed relocation for copper smelting, refineries, asbestos and PVC. In particular, chemical industry and refineries relocate in response to environmental regulation in Western Europe. Leonard (1984) found industries in the copper, zinc and

---

18 This may be explained partly by the fact that many multinationals apply the same high environmental standards in LDCs as used in their home operations. Multinationals may fear aquiring a bad reputation if they apply low standards. For this argument, see UNCTAD (1995, p. 17) on a country case study for Columbia.

lead sectors to be subject to relocation. In another study, Walter (1982) named copper smelters, petroleum refineries, asbestos plants and ferroalloy plants as possible candidates for relocation.

Summarizing the results of the empirical studies, no systematic evidence could be found to support the theory that the stringency of environmental regulation has an effect on the pattern of specialization in international trade or on location decisions of firms. It is suspected that the main reason is the size of compliance costs. For all but the most heavily polluting industries, the cost of complying is only a small fraction of the total cost of production. In cases where trade patterns and location decisions seem to react to environmental regulation, other factors may be the cause of relocation rather than environmental regulation itself. Jaffe et al. (1995) claim that a country's stage of development may be the major cause of the observed concentration of dirty industries in LDCs. LDCs, in a take-off stage of development, are characterized by pollution-intensive steel production and other heavy industries. In developed countries, these industries were replaced by high-tech and service industries.

> It is by no means clear that the changes in trade patterns were caused by increasingly strict environmental regulations in developed countries. The observed changes in international trading patterns are consistent with the general process of development in the Third World. As countries develop, manufacturing accounts for a larger portion of their economic activity. (Jaffe et al., 1995, p. 146)[19]

2.3 THE POLITICAL ECONOMY OF TRADE AND THE ENVIRONMENT

The theoretical and empirical literature does not find systematic evidence that environmental policies have major effects on trade patterns or on location decisions of producers. Therefore, Perroni and Wigle (1994) conclude that the link between trade and the environment barely exists or at least is

19 Other authors explicitly consider the case of LDCs specializing in dirty products for environmental cost reasons (Grossman, 1995). As the environment in higher-developed countries improves through strict environmental regulation, LDCs fill the demand for products from environmentally demanding production. However, it seems that environmental improvements in industrial countries result not only from such composition effects but from cleaner technologies applied in the sectors of production. In Germany, for instance, the major environmental improvements reflect a change in the composition of output only to a small degree. For example, the improvement in river-water quality stems from new production and clean-up technologies of chemical and paper producers, for instance. The drastic reduction of SO_2 emissions is the result of government laws, requiring shrubbers in coal-fired power plants.

overestimated. Consequently, one of the prominent authors in this field, Scott Barrett, suggests that politicians should refrain from the strategic use of environmental policy, a conclusion for which there is broad agreement among economists (Barrett, 1994, p. 328):

> These theoretical findings are as ambivalent as those appearing in the empirical literature. Taken together, they suggest that the incentives for governments to behave strategically in devising environmental policy are limited.

However, in reality, politicians are not interested in the normative prescriptions of economists, as the abundance of inefficient trade and environmental policies suggests. Public choice provides a different approach. Self-interested politicians interact with pressure groups, for example to improve their chances of winning the coming elections. With regard to the trade–environment discussion, public choice argues that environmental policies may not always cause a decline in output and profits, as the standard theory, reviewed above, suggests. Environmental regulation may be favored by producers for two reasons. First, certain types of environmental regulation have a direct protectionist impact and are therefore attractive for producers. Second, there are measures which are indirectly protectionist. Environmental measures may have harmful effects on the competitiveness of producers, but these measures facilitate the lobbying for trade protection.

In this regard, Leidy and Hoekman (1994) found that three of the five US industries identified as pollution intensive by Tobey (1990), are heavily protected as well. These industries are chemicals, paper and pulp, and primary iron and steel. Leidy and Hoekman (1994, p. 242) conclude:

> the effects on trade patterns expected by Tobey (and others) need not emerge because new trade barriers which tend to offset such effects may be induced by environmental policy. Thus Tobey may be measuring the status-quo preserving effects of endogenous protection rather than the trade-altering effects of pollution control ceteris paribus.

Leidy and Hoekman find that environmental measures can facilitate the granting of trade protection, but conversely, public choice analysis can be applied to explain how trade measures are accompanied by environmental regulation as well. Environmental policy, similar to trade policy, is subject to the discretion of politicians and open to the demands of pressure groups. This approach, the political economy of the environment, is presented in Subsection 2.3.1. An extension on an open-economy setting discussing trade and environment issues, is given in Subsection 2.3.2.

2.3.1 The Political Economy of the Environment

The political economy of the environment[20] explains why environmental policy is chosen in the manner actually observed rather than how it should be optimally chosen. Political economy states that efficiency considerations are less important in determining economic policy than the redistribution of income and wealth. All political agents, that is, voters, politicians, interest groups and public bureaucrats, are modeled as rational and self-interested utility maximizers. However, not all political agents are decisive for the political outcome. Voters are assumed to be rationally ignorant in a representative democracy. They choose to remain uninformed since costs for obtaining political information are high. Rationally ignorant voters allow politicians to gain discretionary power which they can use to create and distribute rents.

This book investigates environmental policy making in a representative democracy because most Western democracies are representative in nature. The median-voter concept, although popular, seems to have more explanatory power in direct democracies.[21] Furthermore, this study will confine itself to work with a type of interest-group models, the political-support-function approach, as this is a standard concept in the theory of regulation.[22] Following Stigler (1971) and Peltzman (1976), it is assumed that the elected politician pursues a policy which maximizes his or her political support. It is assumed that political support, earned by the policy maker, depends on the gainers and losers of the pursued policy. Thus, the policy maker balances the marginal gains of political support from the gainers against the marginal losses of political support from the losers.[23]

The level of environmental regulation

One question the political economy of the environment attempts to answer regards the level of environmental regulation. Why does one often observe

---

20 This draws from Ursprung (1992). For some of the issues mentioned, see Hahn (1990), Frey et al. (1991) and Weck-Hannemann (1994).

21 For an application of the median-voter model to trade policy, see Mayer (1984) and Weck-Hannemann (1992); for an application to international capital movements, see Schulze (1996).

22 A number of other approaches to modeling the political process are surveyed by Ursprung (1991). An overview on public choice analysis is given by Bernholz and Breyer (1993, 1994), and Mueller (1989).

23 The political support function is rather an ad hoc concept but there are attempts to provide a microeconomic foundation. Grossman and Helpman (1994) model the channels through which interest groups attempt to influence the incumbent government. In their model, interest groups make offers for political contributions which depend on government policies. Afterwards the government sets policies with regard to its own objectives and collects the contributions. In equilibrium, neither the interest groups nor the government have an incentive to deviate from their positions.

inefficiently lax environmental regulation, why sometimes (probably more seldom) inefficiently strict regulation? Since pollution standards are prevalent to combat pollution from production, a standard is used as an example to illustrate the consequences of environmental policy. The simplest scenario imaginable includes only producers, consumers of goods and consumers of the environment. As a result of the pollution standard, producers face increasing costs of production. Therefore, producers will oppose the standard. Since the price of the good rises as a consequence of the standard, consumers oppose the standard as well. There is a second class of consumers, the consumers of the environment. They support the standard to profit from a cleaner environment.

The resulting standard depends on the political power of the three interests. Political power depends on the ability of these three interests to organize powerful pressure groups for public goods, that is, environmental regulation. Olson (1965) identifies three conditions which make political organization possible: first, a small number of actors with intensive preferences; second, the supply of private goods of the umbrella organization; and third, compulsion.

The *producers* of the dirty good suffer substantial losses if the pollution regulation is introduced. The number of domestic producers is often quite small. These interests can be organized easily, according to Olson's first condition. The *consumers of the dirty good* may also suffer a substantial loss as a consequence of the pollution regulation. Since the number of the consumers is much larger than the number of domestic producers, consumers can be expected to be less organized than producers. The ability of the *consumers of the environment* to organize depends on the type of pollution. If pollution is less visible and tends to damage the environment at large, organization will be difficult. However, locally concentrated pollution or visible damages (*Waldsterben*) tend to improve their ability to organize. If pollution is locally concentrated, the number of the consumers of the environment can be small enough to allow for organization, according to Olson's first condition. For pollution issues which are not locally concentrated but visible, some problems of organization can be overcome since environmental umbrella groups supply private goods to attract members, such as nature magazines or insurance for bicyclists; this is the second Olsonian condition.

The producers of the dirty good represent a powerful interest group against environmental regulation. Organized environmental interests represent a powerful counter-lobby who press for stricter regulation. Therefore, the overall level of environment policy can hardly be predicted because it depends on the specifics of each case of regulation and on the relative strength of pressure groups involved. Environmental standards are inefficiently low if the causal chain linking production, emission and environmental damage in the production process is a particularly complicated one. Then, environmentalists have a hard time being politically successful. On the other hand, if the pollution issue is particularly visible, for example, waste and recycling issues, regulation may be much stricter than the results of the normative economic analysis recommend.[24]

Furthermore, another condition is helpful to obtain a strict environmental policy. In contrast to the example above, certain industries may gain from strict regulation. This occurs in the case of asymmetrical distribution of regulatory effects among different groups of firms. In the manner of raising rivals' cost,[25] firms may obtain a competitive advantage because their competitors have difficulties complying with the proposed regulatory measure. Along with environmentalists, these producers may form an implicit coalition to raise regulation beyond normative demands.

The choice of the instrument for environmental protection

The second question the political economy of the environment addresses is the choice of the instruments for environmental protection. The environmental policy instruments most frequently implemented are technology standards and quantitative constraints on the emission of pollutants. The question arises as to why these regulatory instruments are more popular than the more efficient non-regulatory instruments such as pollution taxes and emission certificates. Again, the focus is on the two most crucial interest groups shaping pollution policies, organized producers and environmentalists.

Organized producers profit from regulatory instruments for three reasons: rent creation, rent shifting and rent protection. Buchanan and Tullock (1975) show that a perfectly competitive industry can obtain rents through an environmental policy limiting output, but not with a pollution tax. Prior to regulation, perfect competition ensures that production takes place at minimal cost, prices equal minimal cost and, consequently, profits are zero. A pollution tax increases costs and drives up prices until the price equals marginal cost. In the post-regulation equilibrium, profits are again zero. The case is different if the environmental policy limits output: now production

---

24 The case in which we definitely do not observe adequate environmental policy concerns transboundary and global pollution issues (pollution of the seas, ozone depletion, global warming, destruction of the rain forests). When domestic pollution issues are at stake we observe a balance of pressure groups pro and contra environmental regulation. This balance does not hold for international pollution issues. One explanation may be that 'greens' in different countries face an international prisoner's dilemma which leads to inefficiently low environmental regulation (for the greens' prisoner's dilemma, see also Subsection 2.3.2).

25 This term is from Salop and Scheffman (1983).

takes place at a higher price than average cost; consequently profits are earned. The regulatory measure *creates rents* by limiting competition, *shifts rents* from consumers and from the public tax receipts to the producers, and finally, *protects rents* by limiting entry.[26] The fact that regulatory environmental measures increase profits can be shown for non-competitive industry structures as well. An environmental tax raises costs and lowers profits in oligopoly. An output constraint, however, may increase profits. With the help of the output constraint, the oligopolists create a cartel, which otherwise could not be enforced. Again, higher profits can only be sustained if entry of competitors is strictly restrained.[27]

At the first glance, the environmentalists, the second decisive group shaping pollution regulation, do not seem to be consistently in favor of one type of instrument over the other. Their sole interest is the protection of the environment. However, they may simply want to support the strongest interest group – the producers – in order to make sure that some environmental policy measure – standards – is taken at all. Considering the coalition of interests favoring regulatory measures over free market instruments, it becomes clear why environmental politics has, in practice, so little in common with the normative prescriptions of economists.[28]

2.3.2 The Influence of Environmental Concerns on Trade Policy

How does environmentalism affect trade policies? The analysis on trade and the environment reviewed in Section 2.2, attempts to find evidence regarding the possibility of eco-dumping: does international competition induce a rat race that is driving down environmental standards to inefficiently low levels? As explained above, neither the empirical nor the theoretical literature come to clear-cut conclusions. The theoretical literature reviewed concludes that trade considerations may either drive environmental regulation below efficient levels or may as well drive them above efficient levels. Moreover,

---

26 Maloney and McCormick (1982) show that this argument holds not only for output constraints, but for regulations restricting pollution as well.

27 Dewees (1983) presents various examples of discriminating new pollution sources.

28 The slow emergence of market-based instruments for environmental protection, seems to contradict the conclusion. Only if market-based instruments are not applied in their pure form do they become, for the same reasons as standards, attractive in the political process. At the same time they lose the efficiency properties desired by economists. Environmental taxes may be applied with a considerable number of exceptions for 'severely affected' producers. Earmarking of environmental taxes may generate considerable support from environmentalists. Tradable emission permits may be attractive for producers when they grandfather current pollution levels. Grandfathering may erect market barriers for potential entrants and, therefore, reduce competition. All these measures increase the leeway for politicians and bureaucrats and disturb by no means their chances of 'seeking rents by setting rents'. For a political-economy discussion of market-based solutions for environmental protection, see Weck-Hannemann (1994).

there is barely any empirical evidence that the phenomenon of eco-dumping has some significance.

The political-economic approach asks a different question regarding the link between trade and environmental policies: is the environment used to facilitate the protectionist ambitions of producers? This issue became prominent under the label 'eco-protectionism'.[29] Research on endogenous policy making considers how political pressure groups shape environmental regulation for trade policy reasons. In this subsection, there are two issues to be explored. First, how do *producer interests* shape environmental regulation for trade policy reasons? The case of producer preferences for inefficient instruments of environmental protection and for environmental product regulation is considered. Second, the likely impact of organized *environmental interests* on trade policy is investigated.

Environmental product standards as means of achieving trade protection

In contrast to environmental process standards, the regulation of adverse effects of consumption with product standards has different effects on producers.[30] Domestic product standards have to be obeyed not only by domestic producers, but also by their foreign competitors when supplying the domestic market.[31] Domestic producers may favor this kind of regulation if obeying the standards induces significantly higher costs for their foreign competitors. One such example is packaging regulations, in which certain types of packaging and recycling rules may be easier for domestic producers to obey than for their foreign competitors (see GATT, 1993a). Usually, foreign competitors face higher compliance costs because information about the standard may be more difficult to obtain abroad.

Underlying protectionist motivations are suspected for several environmental product standards. However, it is nearly impossible to prove whether the relevant environmental product standard is motivated by environmental or by protectionist intentions (see Laplante and Garbalt, 1992). The Danish Bottle Case, in which Denmark prohibited the use of metal containers for beer and soft drinks, is one of the conspicuous cases. Big foreign producers face higher compliance costs than local producers since the former have to transport the bulky recyclable containers over long distances to Denmark. Taking-back and recycling obligations for old cars, introduced in Germany, are suspected of having protectionist motivations as well. The

---

29   There are no empirical investigations on eco-protectionism. One exception is Grasstek (1992), who explores voting in the US Congress on trade and environment policies.
30   For an analysis of eco-protectionism with product standards, see Körber (1997).
31   It is assumed, as required by international trade law, that foreign and domestic producer face the *same* product standards on the domestic market.

same suspicion is held for the corporate average fuel efficiency regulations in the US, which limit fuel consumption per mile for the average sold car of each producer in the US. Corporate Average Fuel Efficiency regulations benefit US producers because only European luxury car producers were fined for exceeding the regulations in recent years (see Bommer, 1996b).

Inefficient environmental regulation as means for obtaining trade protection

In the preceding subsection, it was argued that – in a closed economy – producers favor inefficient environmental instruments for the reasons of rent creation, rent shifting and rent protection. In an open economy, inefficient environmental instruments may even be more advantageous for import-competing producers because they may be helpful for obtaining trade protection. Leidy and Hoekman (1994) extend the analysis of Buchanan and Tullock (1975), who explain rent creation by environmental regulation, by considering the case of an open economy (see the preceding subsection).

Leidy and Hoekman (1994) discuss how inefficient environmental policies help to enhance the probability for trade protection if administrative protection rules are in place. First, they argue that a formal institutional setting, necessary to implement and supervise environmental standards, creates space for cooperative behavior. Regulation is the Olsonian third condition 'compulsion' which helps to bring a large number of producers together. This enables import-competing firms to cooperate and lobby together for trade protection. Second, they argue that this formal institutional setting allows for the inclusion of foreign firms and may induce voluntary export restraints.[32] Third, environmental standards help to raise market entrance barriers. Therefore, protection is even more attractive for firms. Rents from protection are not dissipated over time because of barriers to entry. This is rent protection. Fourth, environmental standards may ease the showing of 'injury'. The injury criterion of US-administered protection allows for trade restrictions if US producers face layoffs or declining market shares, which are due to a surge in imports. For example, a decline in domestic producers' sales after new environmental regulation is instituted, helps to limit foreign producers' access to the domestic market.

The impact of environmentalists on trade protection

After analyzing the interests of producers in environmental policy making to gain a protectionist international trade policy, we focus on the impact of environmental pressure groups on the determination of international trade

---

32 In contrast to tariffs, voluntary export restraints (VERs) may benefit foreign producers since they create rents by restraining competition. See Hillman and Ursprung (1988) on the choice between tariffs and VERs as a means of protection.

policy. When considering a model of political competition, Hillman and Ursprung (1994) have considered the circumstances under which environmental interests are agents of either free trade or protectionism. They show how the trade-policy outcome depends on whether the source of environmental damage is in production or consumption, and whether or not environmentalists care only about the environment of their home countries or about the foreign environment as well. In this analysis, the sole policy instrument is trade policy.

First, the case is considered in which environmentalists do not influence trade policy making. Hillman and Ursprung (1994) show that the policy equilibrium consists of a polarization of both candidates' policy positions. Depending on his constituency – producers who either gain or lose from a tariff – one candidate announces a protectionist platform. The other candidate promises free trade. If environmental interests enter into the political arena, the equilibrium of political competition – polarized policy positions – is unaltered. The question is, which candidate do the environmentalists support and, therefore, which policy platforms – free trade or protection – are improved?

When the adverse environmental impact is associated with *domestic consumption* and the environmentalists are concerned only with the domestic environment ('greens' according to Hillman and Ursprung, 1994), environmentalists support the protectionist candidate and increase the probability of a protectionist trade policy. Protectionism increases industry concentration, hence, less is produced and the environment is improved. The outcome is unchanged if environmentalists are concerned with global pollution ('super-greens' according to Hillman and Ursprung, 1994). Environmentalists in both countries support their protectionist candidates as protectionism minimizes world production and, in consequence, world pollution.

When the source of the adverse environmental impact is *domestic production*, the situation is more complex and environmentalists confront strategic problems in their choice of which trade policy to support. Greens wish to minimize production at home by 'exporting pollution via trade' (Pethig, 1975). They support the free-trade candidate. Free trade increases imports and, hence, domestic production declines and, finally, the environment is improved. However, greens in both countries act according to this strategy. They face a prisoner's dilemma in mutually polluting themselves via trade. The best outcome for environmentalists in both countries is mutual protectionism, where no country's environmentalists free ride off the other. Since environmentalists from different countries face a coordination problem, they become advocates of free trade. On the other hand, environmentalists who are super-greens do not confront such a prisoner's dilemma when deciding which candidate to support. The super-greens internalize the potential conflicts, since they seek to minimize the total adverse environmental impact associated with international trade in both countries. Hence, the super-greens have no incentive to free ride off each other's imports by supporting protectionist candidates.

2.3.3 Conclusions

Political economy explores the incentives of pressure groups and policy makers to abuse policies for their own selfish interests. Because the focus is on environmental policy making in open, trading economies, we emphasize protectionist interests in the conduct of environmental regulation. This phenomenon is described as eco-protectionism and addresses two issues. First, it was shown that strict environmental product standards can be in the interest of domestic producers. Producers may support the introduction of product standards as an indirect means of trade policy if their foreign competitors have major difficulties in complying. Second, inefficient regulatory instruments may be supported by producers as a means of indirect rent seeking. By showing 'injury' from these regulatory instruments, producers may increase their opportunity to obtain trade protection. Organized environmentalists are also decisive in the environmental-policy outcome. Their motivation being solely environmental protection, environmentalists may join the demands of producers for protectionist environmental policies because restraining trade may be the only way of obtaining environmental protection at all.

The political-economic framework clarifies the importance of considering the motives of major interest groups involved in determining environmental policy. This book explores the trade–environment question from the other perspective: while it was shown how environmental policies can be abused to obtain a protectionist outcome, the remainder analyzes how the abolishment of trade protection influences environmental policy. With protectionist instruments no longer available, industries may search for new ways of creating, shifting and protecting rents via environmental policy. Prior to investigating economic integration and the environment from an endogenous policy perspective in Chapters 4, 5 and 6, the next chapter reviews the literature on the environmental effects of trade which takes environmental policy as given.

APPENDIX 2A: MEASURING THE POLLUTION INTENSITY OF MANUFACTURING

Sectors of production can be classified as dirty or clean according to two different methods which are applied here to determine the pollution intensity of sectors of production and, in Chapter 4, to estimate the environmental impact of NAFTA for the United States. This appendix provides an overview of measuring the environmental impact of manufacturing sectors by PACE and by toxic release data.

PACE

PACE are collected using a questionnaire of the US Department of Commerce (see US Department of Commerce, 1993) and are applied, for example, by Tobey (1990) and Low (1992b). This approach identifies dirty industries as those with the highest PACE per unit of output. PACE include payments to the government, that is, sewage and waste-disposal services, and direct operation costs for air and water-pollution abatement, waste disposal and costs for the depreciation of equipment (see Low, 1992b). Table 2A.1 presents 1988 PACE on a two-digit SIC level, where petroleum and coal products, paper and allied products, and primary metal industries are classified as the most dirty, facing PACE of more than 1 percent of total output.

A more detailed listing on a three-digit SIC level reveals higher PACE for cement (3.17 percent), and pulp mills (2.42 percent), to report only a few. The weighted average for all industries is 0.54 percent, as reported by Low (1992b).

However, the presented approach has its shortcomings. First, compliance costs are obtained by calculating the expense of end-of-pipe technologies. In recent years, integrated environmental technologies, whose costs are more difficult to measure, have become more common. Second, pollution regulation has increased considerably. There are no studies which include data from the most recent regulations. Furthermore, data are available only for US manufacturers and can be applied only with considerable caution to other countries (see Jaffe et al., 1995).

Table 2A.1: Pollution intensity of US manufacturing measured by PACE

SIC	Commodity	PACE in percent of output
206	sugar	0.360
20	food	0.330
22	textiles	0.270
23	apparel	0.270
24	lumber and wood	0.330
25	furniture and fixtures	0.300
26	paper	1.100
27	printing and publishing	0.140
28	chemicals	1.180
30	rubber and plastics	0.300
283	drugs	0.500
284	cleaning and toilet preparations	0.260
291	petroleum refining	1.620
31	leather	0.240
322	glass	0.620
32	stone and clay	0.700
332	iron and steel	1.210
333	nonferrous metals	1.210
34	fabricated metal	0.480
35	machinery and equipment	0.180
362	computing equipment	0.300
36	electrical equipment	0.450
363	household appliances	0.290
367	electric components	0.450
371	motor vehicles and bodies	0.250
37	transportation equipment	0.280
39	miscellaneous manufactures	0.220

Toxic Releases

The second approach to measure the pollution intensity of industries relies on data collected by the US Environmental Protection Agency's Toxic Release Inventory (TRI) which records air, water, underground and solid-waste releases of 320 toxic substances from 15,000 reporting US plants.[33] The toxic release data, recorded for each sector, are divided by the output of the respective sector to obtain toxic release per unit of production. Table 2A.2 lists the emissions of toxic release in pound per $1000 of sectoral output in the US (see US Environmental Protection Agency, 1996). Industries classified as particularly dirty are chemicals and iron, steel and non-ferrous metals, whereas apparel and related products are ranked as the cleanest, according to toxic release data.

However, the toxic release approach also has its shortcomings. Releases are only measured in terms of weight. They are not adjusted with regard to different degrees of toxicity. Moreover, several toxics are omitted and, furthermore, the inventory measures only releases from manufacturing. Finally, as with PACE, toxic release data are available only for US manufacturing and can be applied to other countries only with considerable caution.

33 US law requires all manufacturing firms with ten or more employees which use at least 10,000 pounds of the monitored chemicals to report their annual releases to the Toxic Release Inventory (see Grossman and Krueger, 1993).

Table 2A.2: *Pollution content of US manufacturing measured by toxic release data*

SIC	Commodity	1989 toxic release in pounds per $1000 of 1989 output
20,21	food, kindred products	0.099
22	textile mill products	0.474
23	apparel and related products	0.021
24	lumber and related products	0.501
25	furniture and fixtures	1.670
26	paper and allied products	1.952
27	printing and publishing	0.380
28	chemicals and allied products	7.480
29	petroleum and coal products	0.667
30	rubber and miscellaneous plastics products	1.865
31	leather and leather products	1.381
32	stone, clay and glass products	0.576
33	iron, steel and non-ferrous metals	3.522
34	fabricated metal products	0.838
35	machinery, excluding electrical	0.226
36	electric and electronic machinery	0.519
37	transportation equipment	0.560
38,39	miscellaneous manufactured commodities	0.528
	output (unweighted) average	1.292

3 Economic Integration and the Environment: Theoretical Findings and Empirical Evidence

The most recent steps toward global economic integration, for example, the completed Uruguay Round of the General Agreement on Tariffs and Trade (GATT), result in a significant reduction of tariffs and non-tariff barriers to trade. The effects of free trade on the environment are mostly indirect and occur via a change in production and consumption activities. This chapter reviews studies on the environmental effects of economy-wide trade liberalization and liberalization in specific production sectors.[1] For most of this chapter, environmental regulation is considered to be exogenous with respect to trade policy. This provides the foundation for the exploration of the effects of trade on environmental policy making in the rest of the study.

The chapter distinguishes four categories of environmental effects of trade: scale, product, spatial and composition effects (see Table 3.1).

The emphasis will be on the composition effects of trade for the following two reasons. First, the scale link, although important in the current discussion, is a very indirect one and, therefore, hard to grasp. Hence, Subsection 3.1.1 reviews the empirical literature with the intention of providing only a 'flavor' for the effects, while skipping theoretical approaches. A similar argument holds for product and spatial effects reviewed in Subsections 3.1.2 and 3.1.3. A second reason for emphasizing composition effects is political economic. Composition effects of economic integration have distributional consequences and, thereby, produce gainers and losers. This is the foundation for the endogenous policy analysis, which explores how winners and losers from economic integration may search to redistribute rents via environmental policy.

---

[1] Closely related are effects of economic policy reforms and structural adjustment programs on the environment, which will also be covered to a limited extent. For African case studies, see UNEP (1995).

Table 3.1:   *Summary of the effects of economic integration on the*
environment

Effects of trade liberalization, surveyed in the following sections	Mechanism	Environmental impact
3.1.1 Scale effects	Increasing demand for the environment as a consumption good	Positive
	Growth in output	Negative
	Declining population growth	Positive
3.1.2 Product and techno- logical effects	Easier access to new, resource-saving and green products and technologies	Positive
	Easier access to high-risk products and technologies	Negative
3.1.3 Spatial effects	Decentralization of production mitigates concentrated damage	Positive
	Production according to comparative advantage leads to specialization and to a concentration of damage	Negative
3.2 Composition effects	Clean sectors of production expand relative to dirty sectors	Positive
	Dirty sectors of production ex-pand relative to clean sectors	Negative

3.1   SCALE, PRODUCT AND SPATIAL EFFECTS

3.1.1   Scale Effects

The trade liberalization–growth-environment link is an indirect one and is, therefore, disputable. This subsection considers a two-stage procedure to explore the effects as indicated by Figure 3.1. In the first stage, the trade–growth link is explored. There is consensus in the literature that trade liberalization fosters growth.[2] Jorgenson and Ho (1993, quoted by WTO, 1995a) found efficiency gains of between 1 and 2 percent of GDP and between 3 and 4 percent for countries with severe distortions. The static effects of the European Common Market are estimated to be between 4.5 and 7 percent (see European Commission, 1988). Analyses for the scale effects of NAFTA found small effects for the US and Canada but up to 6.5 percent for Mexico (see Brown et al., 1992b). Dynamic gains of free trade are even larger. Therefore, it seems to be safe to say that free trade increases economic activity.

Figure 3.1:   The trade–growth–environment link

In the second stage, the effects of growth on the environment need to be investigated. Trade-induced growth causes positive and negative effects on the environment. On the one hand, by extending production, growth directly causes more emissions, waste and pollution-intensive transport. In Thailand, for instance, annual average growth between 7 and 8 percent over the last 20 years raised annual hazardous waste creation to 1.9 million tons by the year 1990 and a fourfold increase is expected by the year 2001 (see Repetto, 1994, p. 4). In Thailand's industrial hub, Bangkok, health standards for several air pollutants exceed World Health Organization (WHO) limits (see also Subsection 3.3 on Thailand).

Indonesia is another example of how trade and other policy reforms accelerated the speed of growth and, in consequence, contributed to environmental degradation. Manufacturing output doubled every six to seven years during the 1970s and the 1980s; 1990 manufacturing output was about eight times its 1970 value (see Munasinghe and Cruz, 1995). Consequently, toxic emissions from manufacturing increase with income growth although the industrial pollution intensity declined (see Lucas et al., 1992).

On the other hand, there is an indirect growth effect which alleviates environmental pressure. Growth increases personal income, which results in an increased demand for a wide range of goods. Following Section 2.1, where the environment is considered as a consumption good, growth raises

2   However, there is some skepticism with regard to the empirical validation of the openness–growth link. For a critical comparison of empirical studies, see Pritchett (1996).

the demand for environmental amenities as well. In this regard, the reduction of poverty, one major source of environmental degradation, illustrates the benefits of growth. For instance, poverty causes deforestation as marginalized people become slash-and-burn farmers (see World Bank, 1992). However, for the most part the higher demand for a cleaner environment does not 'automatically' cause higher environmental quality. Since environmental quality is a public good which has to be provided publicly, rising demand for environmental quality needs to be transformed into more restrictive environmental policies. This has to be achieved through the political process. Hence, environmental policy is endogenous not only to the change in composition of the economy, but to growth as well. In this regard, Mexico is quoted as an example where growth led to stricter environmental regulation (see *The Economist*, 1993).[3]

Some empirical studies investigate the relationship between growth and environmental quality. Grossman and Krueger (1993) measure environmental quality by ambient levels of urban air pollution. They rely on a data set from the Global Environmental Monitoring System (GEMS) of WHO and the United Nations Environmental Programme (UNEP). Since 1976, GEMS has monitored the concentrations of several pollutants, that is, SO_2, particulate matter and smoke, in a cross-section of urban areas in 19 to 42 countries, areas regarded as representative regarding geographic conditions in different regions of the world. Grossman and Krueger (1995) also rely on GEMS data to extend the analysis to include water pollution.[4] Since 1979, water pollutants, which include pesticides, heavy metals and basic physical, chemical and micro-biological variables, has been measured in 58 countries. A different set of environmental indicators, those provided by the World Resources Institute, is used by Selden and Song (1994). Emissions of air pollutants are estimated for various countries by multiplying national consumption of fuels with coefficients, which reflect the stringency of national environmental policies.

Grossman and Krueger (1993) analyze the relationship between several pollutants and real GDP per capita. For some of the pollutants they obtain a

3   It seems that the indirect demand effect for environmental quality lags behind the direct output effect, putting a strain on the environment. In the past, environmental policies in the OECD countries only caught up when environmental problems had already caused considerable damage, or industrial accidents (for example, Seveso) made the perils of not handling environmental issues obvious. The rapid industrialization in some LDCs in recent years, particularly in South-East Asia, has caused environmental problems which have not yet been taken care of sufficiently (see Repetto, 1994 and French, 1993).

4   Work on water quality and growth is not surveyed here, also the impact of other air pollutants is not undertaken. Other work includes Shafik and Bandyopadhyay (1992), who found an inverted u-shaped relationship for total and annual deforestation and per-capita income.

bell-shaped 'environmental Kuznets curve': pollution concentrations rise with income, peak at a certain income and decline as income rises further. suspended particulate matter (SPM) concentrations were found to rise with income until there is an annual per-capita income of approximately $5000, and then fall beyond that point. Selden and Song (1994) find a similar bell-shaped relationship between growth and SPM. They calculated the peak of ambient SPM concentrations at a per-capita income of $8000.[5] Regarding SO_2 emissions, Grossman and Krueger (1993) found that emissions reach a peak between $4000 and $5000 of real per-capita income; Selden and Song (1994), again, found a higher turning point ($8643).

However, the turning points are less favorable for other air pollutants. Selden and Song found turning points of $11,338 for carbon monoxide and $22,874 for nitrous oxides. A study by Holtz-Eakin and Selden (1992) did not find a turning point for municipal waste or for CO_2 emissions at all; these pollutants increase steadily with income. As argued in Subsection 2.3.1, political-economic reasons may be the underlying cause for this outcome. One can expect that no turning point would be found for pollutants where the environmental damage effects are complicated and where costs are dispersed. If pollution is particularly visible, the effects are concentrated and easy to identify, environmentalists may push for stricter regulation if a high-growth economy has more resources available. In this case an environmental kuznets curve may be obtained. However, environmentalists have a hard time of being politically successful if the causal chain linking production, emission and environmental damage to the production process is a particularly complicated one.

A final environmental effect of economic growth is declining population growth. Population growth is one of the major causes of pressure on natural resources in urban and rural environments in LDCs. According to a World Bank study, population growth rates tend to decline as income expands (see World Bank, 1992), thereby mitigating pressure on the environment.

3.1.2 Product and Technology Effects

Trade liberalization alters the variety of products available. If free trade makes clean products, for example, water-treatment plants, solar cells or cars equipped with catalytic converters, more readily available, then consumers switch from the environmentally harmful to these clean products, and the environment will benefit. However, free trade may make environmentally

5 Selden and Song (1994) explain their high turning point by the fact that their data measure air pollution not only in urban areas, but all over the country. It is possible that urban pollution in developing countries receives earlier attention and leads to the lower turning point found by Grossman and Krueger (1993).

harmful products more readily available. For instance, there are concerns that trade in hazardous wastes, radioactive substances and pesticides will expand.

Similar to the case of final products, trade liberalization eases the access to foreign technology. This is particularly relevant for developing countries since they rely to a large extent on the technology and equipment produced in the developed countries. Since environmental concerns in developed countries are high, new equipment tends to be more resource-saving and environmentally friendly than old equipment (see Grossman, 1995). This link may contribute to environmental improvements since it alters the environmental impact of a given sectoral composition.

In a study on wood-pulp production, Wheeler and Martin (1992) found that clean pulping technology is adapted more quickly in undistorted and open countries than in protected economies.[6] They found a reduction of 10–12 percent of new pulp-related pollution in open economies. In a different study, Birdsall and Wheeler (1992) report Chile as an example of how the transfer of clean production technology is supported by the degree of openness to trade and investment. Trade liberalization also helped assembly-based industries to shift from pollution-intensive processing sectors to cleaner ones in Indonesia in the 1980s (see IMF, 1994).

3.1.3 Spatial Effects

The environmental impact of the spatial distribution of production draws on the fact that environmental damage usually increases overproportionally as pollution goes up (see Figure 3.2).

The spatial decentralization of production does not, *ceteris paribus*, reduce environmental pollution in total, but alleviates the damage from environmental pollution by shifting production from industrial centers to other regions of a country. Consider the two regions, as drawn in Figure 3.2, in which pollution-intensive production causes damage: the industrialized region A faces high damage from pollution whereas the less-industrialized region B faces less damage due to pollution. Decentralization of production causes a shift of pollution-intensive production from the densely populated and industrialized region A to region B. The shift of production (and therefore of pollution) reduces the pollution impact on the health of the metropolitan population, whereas it increases pollution damage in region B, but to a lesser extent.[7] For instance, before NAFTA came into force,

---

6   Wheeler and Martin (1992) measure the openness of an economy using a price distortion index.
7   These spatial effects bear some proximity to the recent trade and geography discussion, triggered by Paul Krugman. He argues that the spatial distribution of production has to balance increasing returns to scale from concentrated production against higher

assembly-based production sites clustered in *Maquiladoras* on the Mexican side of the border, which caused great pollution problems. NAFTA is expected to induce a more even distribution of economic activities across Mexico.

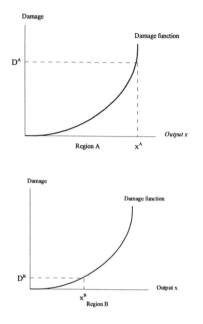

Figure 3.2:   *Different consequences of pollution in two regions*

Indonesia is also an example where the spatial diversification of production may mitigate environmental pressure. In Indonesia, where industrial output has increased eightfold since 1970 and is expected to increase 13-fold by 2020, three-quarters of all industrial production is located on the island of Java (see Repetto, 1994, p. 5). Sixty percent of production on Java is in urban areas, polluting most of the urban surface and groundwater supplies. Air pollution is high as well. For instance, 28 percent of women and children in Jakarta suffer from respiratory disease. Munasinghe and Cruz (see 1995, p. 51) found that liberalization efforts accelerated the growth of dirty sectors of production outside Java. On Java, cleaner assembly activities have grown faster than 'dirtier' processing activities.

transportation cost (Krugman, 1991). Integrating the environment in this framework requires balancing increasing returns to scale of concentrated production against higher transportation cost and higher environmental externalities.

3.2 COMPOSITION EFFECTS

Composition effects derive from the fact that trade liberalization alters the allocation of resources between sectors of production. When the sectoral composition of output changes, the environment is affected since the sectors of production pollute the environment to a different extent.

3.2.1 Theoretical Approaches

In a Heckscher–Ohlin framework of a small open economy, Rauscher (1991a) explores the effects of trade on the environment which result from the change in the composition of economic activity. Purely domestic pollution originates from production and is regulated by a pollution tax. In a set-up with a dirty and a clean good, liberalization of trade increases the production in the dirty good at the expense of the clean good if the small country has a comparative advantage in the dirty good. The expansion of trade increases pollution. If the emission tax is lower than optimal, the efficiency gains from free trade are offset by environmental losses. However, results are reversed if the country has a comparative advantage in the clean good. Free trade causes environmental improvements which reinforce the efficiency gains from trade. López (1994) comes to similar conclusions when considering a small-open-economy framework with the factors capital, labor and environment. He considers a developing country which has a protected polluting manufacturing sector and an exporting primary sector. If primary production has no adverse effects on the environment, trade liberalization improves the environment because the primary sector expands at the expense of dirty manufacturing. However, if primary production causes environmental damage, trade liberalization cannot be associated with an improved environment in any case.

In a general-equilibrium framework similar to that of Merryfield (1988) and McGuire (1982), Copeland and Taylor (1994) explore the environmental effects of free trade in a two-country model with competitive markets and a continuum of goods, which differ in their pollution intensities. The two countries differ only in their endowment with human capital. Environmental policy is positively linked to income. It follows that the country with a higher stock of human capital chooses a stricter environmental policy than the other country. Trade liberalization shifts production of the dirty good to the low income country, whereas the rich country specializes in clean goods. The composition effects of trade depend on the fact that trade is driven entirely by income-induced differences in pollution regulation. Copeland and Taylor (1994) conclude that trade liberalization increases world pollution because dirty production is concentrated in the low-standard country.[8] A related model by Chichilnisky (1994) analyzes the role of property rights for the environmental outcome. Two identical countries differ only in the property rights of the environmental resource: The 'North' has private property, whereas in the 'South' property rights are ill-defined. Free trade has detrimental effects on the environment: even if trade equalizes all factors and goods prices, the 'North' overconsumes the underpriced resource-intensive products from the 'South'.

The theoretical studies presented above found that the environmental impact of trade liberalization rests on the environmental impact of expanding production relative to declining production: pollution increases if expanding export production is pollution intensive relative to shrinking import-competing production. Regarding the global environment, composition effects alter the impact of production on the environment if technologies vary between the countries and, hence, generate pollution to a different extent. The possibility arises that the environment deteriorates because pollution-intensive production moves to the low-standard country.

3.2.2 Empirical Studies

Lucas et al. (1992) estimated the consequences of alternative trade regimes on the composition of production and, hence, on the toxic intensity of manufacturing. They calculated toxic intensities for most countries by using sectoral emission data from the Toxic Release Inventory, dividing sectoral emissions by sectoral output to obtain emission shares. To explore the consequences of alternative trade regimes, they used a price-level-distortion index to measure openness to international trade. They found that the pollution intensity of manufacturing increased in fast-growing closed economies in the 1970s and 1980s. In contrast, the pollution intensity did not change in fast-growing open economies in the 1970s and declined in the 1980s. Birdsall and Wheeler (1992) came to similar conclusions with regard to Latin American countries. They found that openness for trade and investment reduces the pollution intensity of industries.

Munasinghe and Cruz (1995) found that in Indonesia in the 1970s trade liberalization led to the expansion of comparatively dirty materials-processing sectors, whereas trade liberalization helped to expand comparatively clean assembly processes in the 1980s. Therefore, by shifting to a cleaner production structure, the pollution intensity of Indonesian

---

8   In a related model with transboundary externalities, Copeland and Taylor (1995) show that the environmental effects of free trade depend on the income distribution between both countries. If income is very different, free trade does not equalize factor prices and pollution policies. Hence, industries shift to pollution havens and increase pollution.

production was reduced and pollution problems resulting from the growth of the economy mitigated.

Empirical evidence on NAFTA suggests that environmental improvements can be expected from sectoral changes induced by NAFTA. Mexico has a comparative advantage in comparatively clean labor-intensive production, whereas the US specializes in the production of, relatively dirty, capital-intensive goods, such as electricity production and chemicals (see Grossman and Krueger, 1993, and the empirical work in Chapter 4). Free trade under NAFTA should cause the specialization of both countries into their fields of comparative advantage: the US is expected to specialize into comparatively dirty capital-intensive production, whereas Mexico should concentrate on comparatively clean labor-intensive processes. Since environmental standards are higher in the US than in Mexico, the concentration of dirty production in the high standard country (US) could lower total pollution emitted in both countries. This evidence contradicts the predictions from Copeland and Taylor (1994) who expect low-standard countries to specialize in dirty production.

For developing countries, the liberalization of world trade provides an opportunity to eliminate *tariff escalation* in developed-country markets. Tariff escalation denotes *ad-valorem* tariffs which rise with the processing level of raw materials, for example, the Multi-Fiber Agreement regulating the international trade of textiles. A decline in tariff escalation is the result of the completed Uruguay Round of trade negotiations (see GATT, 1994 and WTO, 1995a).[9] Tariff escalation favors the expansion of downstream processing industries in importing countries and induces the specialization of developing countries in the export of unprocessed raw materials. In LDCs, where about half of all exports still comprise fuels, minerals and other primary commodities (see Repetto, 1994), this has led to massive environmental problems in the primary sectors of forestry, mining, fisheries and agriculture. The elimination of tariff escalation provides the opportunity to mitigate the environmental impact by the diversification of production into sectors, in which developing countries have a comparative advantage. Developing countries could ease environmental pressure if they specialize in labor-intensive production, which is often comparably environmentally friendly (see WTO, 1995a, pp. 12–13).

Sectoral studies

Agriculture is a sector in which environmental problems go hand in hand with trade-distortive policies. Market-access restrictions, export subsidies, domestic agricultural support or high agricultural taxation are abundant. In

---

9   However, in major developed-country markets the level of tariff escalation has increased for a number of products, for example, rubber, jute, lead, zinc, hides, skins and leather.

the prevalence of these two types of distortions, some authors (for example, Anderson, 1992b) see the opportunity of a double dividend of trade liberalization in agriculture: they suggest that trade liberalization will raise farming efficiency by abolishing distortive policies, while environmental externalities could be mitigated at the same time.

The literature, however, paints a mixed picture.[10] Liberalization eases the abolishion of agricultural export subsidies in developed countries, which will drive the world market prices of agricultural commodities up (see Anderson, 1992a and Lutz, 1992). The environmental impact in industrial countries is expected to be positive since a reduction in the use of fertilizers and agro-chemicals follows the decline in agricultural output. On the other hand, abolishing export subsidies for agricultural commodities in developed countries drives world market prices up and may contribute to an intensification of agriculture and to an expansion of production areas in developing countries (see Lutz, 1992). This may result in negative environmental effects.

A shift of cropping patterns towards the expansion of export crops is found to have beneficial effects on soil erosion. In Sub-Saharan Africa, Repetto (1989) found that export crops cause less soil erosion than locally consumed crops do. In West Africa, export tree and bush crops, for example coffee and cocoa, resulted in between two and three times less soil erosion than locally consumed crops, such as maize, yam and cassava, did. For Malawi, Cromwell and Winpenny (1991) found that adjustment-related reforms altered the product variety to soil-improving crops. In a study on the Ivory Coast, López (1995) found less erosion and less biomass loss due to trade liberalization. He distinguishes between two types of crops. Annual crops,

---

10 Abolishing non-trade distortions with negative environmental effects, such as subsidies for agricultural inputs, undoubtedly improves the environment while contributing to efficiency improvements (see Anderson, 1992b). Abolishing subsidies on fertilizers and agro-chemicals mitigates water pollution. A stop on subsidies on water for irrigation avoids water shortages. In general, reducing the subsidization of inputs avoids soil erosion and deforestation, caused by extended farming and ranching and reduced fallow periods (see Runge, 1993). Similar effects are found by Sen (1994) for the fisheries sector, where production subsidies all over the world, such as the support of fishing fleets, contribute to overfishing. The positive impact of these measures on the environment is obvious, but they are only indirectly trade related. Regarding energy use, Burgess (1990) expects sizable environmental benefits from the world-market pricing of energy in Eastern Europe, India and China. As a result of world-market pricing, he expects a fall in worldwide CO_2 emissions by 3 percent. Hughes (1990) estimates a reduction of up to 40 percent in CO_2 emissions in Eastern Europe due to world-market pricing. Anderson (1992b) analyzes the liberalization of coal markets. Assuming constant consumer prices in Europe, he found that coal production in Europe declined. Coal world-market prices would rise with environmentally friendly consequences: demand would shift to less-damaging sources of energy and to lower emissions.

mostly for domestic consumption, are protected from foreign competition. Tree crops, mostly for export, are taxed. He found that liberalization would cause a reduction of the area cultivated, which is not fully compensated by the expansion of tree crop cultivation.

However, some studies found adverse effects of trade liberalization on the environment. According to an empirical study by López (1998), the reduction of agricultural export taxes, for example for cocoa, in Ghana had adverse effects to the environment. He found that the increase of output by the extension of cultivated land and reduced fallow periods increased soil erosion and resulted in a considerable loss of biomass. Progressive liberalization due to a continued reduction of export taxes on some agricultural products while the reduction of import protection on others, may cause a further loss of biomass and a reduction of agricultural productivity. He concludes that the loss in biomass is likely to more than off-set the positive income effects obtained through reducing trade distortions. In a study on Sudan, Stryker et al. (1989) found that trade and other adjustment-related reforms caused considerable deforestation. Higher producer prices for crops encouraged forest clearing for crop production. Amelung and Diehl (1991) link deforestation to the expansion of cattle ranching for export in Mexico and Brazil.

A further concern is the impact of *trade in logs and other wood products* on deforestation of tropical rain forests. Barbier (1994) found that timber trade has not been an important cause for the conversion of forest lands into land for cash-cropping. Domestic factors, that is, distorted prices and subsidies, played a more crucial role. Braga (1992) claims that the Indonesian export ban on logging was unsuccessful because it lowered the price of saw logs and raised home demand for saw logs. With a lower price of logs, he argues, forest resources are less valuable and will, therefore, be less likely to be preserved carefully.

What is the impact of free trade on the protection of *wildlife and endangered species*? Some authors claim that international trade may contribute to sustainable management of endangered species by raising the market prices of endangered species (Barbier et al., 1990; Burgess, 1991; Dohlman, 1990). However, the underlying assumption is that at least rudimentary property rights of natural resources are in place. If there are no property rights, a high market price of wildlife, caused by international trade, would have the opposite effect. By increasing incentives for harvesting and hunting, trade may cause the 'tragedy of the commons',[11] the overexploitation of endangered species and a higher probability of extinction. In a case study on the Philippines, Cruz and Repetto (1993) conclude that the

11   This term is attributed to Hardin (1968).

removal of export restrictions could induce a substantial increase of deforestation.

International trade relies heavily on *transport* capacities. International transport consumes one-eighth of world oil production (see WTO, 1995a, quoting Madeley, 1992). Trade liberalization is responsible for more long-distance transport than the amount of transport for production supplying only the domestic market requires (see Landis Gabel, 1994). Causing an increase in transport, trade liberalization can be made responsible for energy-related environmental damage, mostly air pollution. In this regard, a study on the environmental effects of European integration found that the Common Market is expected to increase truck traffic by 30–50 percent, which would cause more air pollution, see Task Force, 1990; see also Chapter 5). In an empirical study of the effects of European integration on transport, Landis Gabel (1992) found not only that transport increased with free trade, but also that the modal split of traffic shifted to more environmentally harmful modes of transport. Trade causes a shift in the means of transport from sea and rail, which are relatively resource saving, to the more damaging road and air transport. But there is a countervailing effect: increasing trade not only gives rise to more transport and more pollution, but it contributes to a more efficient resource allocation as well, which may improve the environment. For instance, trade liberalization may allow Moroccan tomatoes on the German market to compete with Dutch tomatoes. On the one hand, Moroccan tomatoes cause pollution from long-distance road transport, but heating-oil savings of tomatoes grown in the Moroccan fields instead of in the Dutch greenhouses reduce pollution.

After the various effects of trade on the environment have been reviewed, a country case study on Thailand is presented. This study illustrates the whole range of effects within one country – scale, product, spatial and composition effects. In particular, this case study shows how trade policies lead to the expansion of some sectors, while other sectors contract. This is the foundation for the political-economic analysis undertaken below.

3.3 TRADE LIBERALIZATION AND THE ENVIRONMENT IN A FAST-GROWING LDC ECONOMY: A CASE STUDY FOR THAILAND[12]

Thailand serves as an example of a high-growth developing economy where different trade policies have affected the Thai environment over the last 30

---

12   The sub-section is based on Bommer (1996a).

years.[13] This example reveals the complexity of the effects of trade on the environment. Three periods of trade policy can be distinguished. In the 1960s and early 1970s, the emphasis was on import substitution. From the mid-1970s to the end of the 1980s, a period of export orientation with massive export promotion followed. Since then, as a result of tariff reductions brought about by the Uruguay Round, it was determined that the average applied import tariff level would be reduced from 30 percent to 17 percent by 1997. Furthermore, there has been a redirection of the investment incentives away from export-related incentives to regional development, with all remaining export-related incentives to be phased out by the year 2002 (see WTO, 1995b).

In the first period, the export pattern, dominated by agriculture, put pressure on Thailand's natural resource base. This resulted in deforestation and a long-term decline of soil fertility. The environmental effects of agricultural production for export are difficult to separate from the effects of production for domestic use. Adverse effects of agriculture in Thailand have been felt over a long period. In the last 30 years, the rapid expansion of production of cash crops, for example tapioca, in the east, lower north and northeast regions has been responsible, at least in part, for the rapid deforestation experienced in those regions, and in the northeast in particular. This deforestation had significant short- and long-term effects on the local environment, including the loss of biodiversity and an increase in soil erosion. Logs, which topped the list of commodity exports in the past, are closely linked to deforestation. The percentage of forest land of the total land area in Thailand has shrunk from 53 percent in the 1960s to 26 percent today. Apart from the export of logs, cash-crop production of various agricultural commodities, such as corn, sorghum and tapioca, has contributed to deforestation.

In the second trade-policy period, lasting from the mid-1970s until the end of the 1980s, Thai domestic and foreign investment promotion caused exports to diversify. Manufactured products became the major export commodities. The result on the environment was mixed (see World Bank, 1994). There is evidence that a large share of domestic and foreign investment promoted by the Thai Board of Investment (BOI) was undertaken in relatively pollution-intensive, that is, hazardous-waste-producing, sectors such as metals, metal products and chemicals (see Table 3.2).

13 Since the mid-1980s, Thailand was one of the world's fastest-growing economies with growth averaging over 11.5 percent in the four years to 1990 and 8 percent in the following four years. Real GNP increased fourfold between 1970 and 1990.

Table 3.2:   Foreign direct investment in Thailand

Sector	FDI in billion Baht in 1986–89	Total government-promoted investment in 1986–89
Electrical machinery	37.7	24.4
Transportation equipment	4.2	11.1
Metals	11.6	16.1
Chemicals	10.6	18.0
Total FDI	**64.1**	**69.6**

Source: World Bank, 1994.

Shrimp production helped to diversify Thai exports but caused detrimental effects on the environment. Because of a strong overseas demand, production increased almost tenfold between 1980 and 1990, and in the 1990s at rates of more than 20 percent annually. Thailand became the most important shrimp-producing nation in the region, accounting for 15 percent of world production of cultured shrimps. Support included subsidized diesel, soft loans and investment breaks. One main environmental problem of shrimp production is land clearance. There is notable clearance of mangrove forests, the centerpiece of coastal ecosystems. It was estimated that between 1979 and 1986, 38.3 percent of total mangrove clearance was undertaken for coastal aquaculture purposes, most of which was for shrimp farming. A second concern is saltwater intrusion to freshwater aquifers and shrimp pond effluent discharges. The abstraction of freshwater from underground aquifers for intensive farming in Thailand has resulted in saltwater intrusion and salinization of freshwater aquifers.

In the third period, which started in the early 1990s, investment promotion by the BOI provides incentives to encourage business relocation outside of Thailand's Bangkok Metropolitan Region (BMR). This eases environmental pressures in the BMR.[14] The rural sector is moving towards greater diversification of crops and to non-farm opportunities. In many areas of the country formerly covered with paddies, rice is no longer produced. Some of the land has been devoted to other crops. But the more recent diversification

14 Within the BMR, investment incentives are given for export production only. In the intermediate area of ten provinces a broader range of investment measures is subsidized. In the outer provinces, or 'Zone 3', subsidies are double those for the intermediate area and include subsidized infrastructure projects. Additionally, restrictions on foreign investment were eased in 1995. These measures supporting decentralization have borne fruit. In 1995, almost nine out of ten investments approved by the BOI were in Zone 3 (see *The Economist*, 1996).

also causes environmental problems. One example is the production of ginger in Chiang Rai. Ginger requires new land for cultivation each season, making it a cause of deforestation. In 1989, to stop deforestation, Thailand imposed a ban on logging, turning Thailand from a net exporter to a net importer of logs and sawn timber. In 1994, Thailand's exports of logs and sawn timber were insignificant, comprising only 7.56 percent of total imports of these commodities. Today, mainly sawn timber is exported. The increasingly scarce wood has been replaced by parawood, obtained from clearing over-matured rubber trees in preparation for new plantations. Chips and sawdust are reused for products such as particle board.

This case study illustrates how trade policies affected the Thai environment. Scale effects put considerable pressure on the environment, which was exacerbated by import-substitution and export-promotion trade policies. Free-trade policy seems to mitigate the congestion effects of centralized production. In the last few years, the positive effects of growth, increasing the demand for a clean environment, seem to have come into effect. Environmental polices, for example the ban on logging, seem to catch up, but with a considerable lag.

3.4 TOWARD A POLITICAL ECONOMY OF ECONOMIC INTEGRATION AND THE ENVIRONMENT

The empirical and theoretical literature on economic integration and the environment, as reviewed above, confirms neither the fears of trade critics nor the hopes of free-trade advocates. Trade critics warned about a deterioration of the environment since increasing competition between countries may drive down environmental standards and increases output and pollution-intensive transport. Free-trade advocates hope that free trade improves the environment. They believe that the efficiency properties of free trade make the use of the environment more efficient.

The theoretical studies found that the environment improves only if free trade expands relatively clean export production while shrinking relatively dirty import-competing production. Empirical evidence finds the latter case to hold for LDCs. These studies find that open LDCs tend to have a more environment-friendly structure of production than relatively closed LDC economies. Studies, however, which analyze the effects of liberalization in single sectors of production come to rather ambivalent conclusions.

Public choice provides a different approach by focusing on the endogenous determination of environmental policy. Trade policies not only affect the environment in the various ways presented, but they affect environmental policies as well. The underlying reason is that free trade alters the composition of the economy and, thereby, affects the stakes of the interest groups. With the abolition of trade protection, import-competing sectors confronted with foreign competition may suffer heavy losses. These sectors may be compensated by the means of environmental regulation for their losses. Policy makers rely on environmental regulation to redistribute some of the gains of free trade, received by certain groups, to the losers of free trade. This book focuses on the sectoral effects of economic integration because the expansion and contraction of sectors of production are nothing more than distributional effects affecting the major interest groups, the producers. Hence, environmental policy may become a substitutive policy instrument for trade protection as tariffs and other border regulations are no longer available under free trade. The few pieces of research considering environmental policy as endogenous to trade policy are reviewed below.

In a model of perfect competition, Ludema and Wooton (1994) examine the environmental consequences of free trade in a non-cooperative game between two countries. Their analysis is related to the terms-of-trade approaches reviewed in Subsection 2.2.1, which found that countries increase environmental regulation if their export products are pollution intensive. In Ludema and Wooton's set-up, country 1 and country 2 produce good X, whereby only country 1 exports the good to country 2. Production of good X in country 1 causes environmental externalities in country 2. Furthermore, they assume that the good is neither consumed in country 1, nor are there any externalities in this country. Both countries rely on trade policies to exert monopoly power: country 1 levies an export tariff to increase the producer price of the good whereas country 2 levies an import tariff to improve its terms-of-trade and to reduce the pollution externality caused by foreign production. In a free-trade agreement, the first-best instrument of improving terms of trade, the tariff, is not available. But countries choose environmental regulation to exert terms of trade effects. The competition between the two governments to exploit monopoly power results in particularly restrictive environmental regulation in both countries. The consequence is a low level of pollution and a low level of trade.

Rauscher (1991b) explores the effects of capital-market liberalization on environmental regulation. He also considers a setting of perfect competition where two countries set their environmental taxes non-cooperatively. In contrast to Ludema and Wooton (1994), he considers capital-market liberalization rather than trade liberalization. Both countries produce one good with the production factors environment and capital. They differ only in their endowment with capital. Restricted international capital mobility limits the international transfer of capital. Hence rental costs are not equalized. An environmental tax has two effects. It internalizes externalities of pollution and affects the rental rate of capital. The capital-rich country chooses a lenient tax to increase the productivity of capital, which reduces capital exports and increases the rental rate. The capital-poor country has an interest in a low interest rate because it has to pay for the capital imports. Hence, it levies a strict pollution tax to decrease the productivity of capital. This decreases capital imports and finally results in a lower rental rate. Capital-market liberalization increases capital transfers from the country that is well endowed with capital to the country that is poorly endowed. For the country that is well endowed with capital, the effects on the environment are positive. As capital moves away, the productivity of the production factor environment declines and emissions fall. Moreover, rising income increases the demand for the environment and, therefore, causes a stricter environmental tax. The effects on the country that is poorly endowed with capital are ambiguous. While income effects cause a stricter environmental tax, the rising productivity of the environment may drive up emissions.

These two studies are rather specific, but they give a first taste of how strategic motivations of governments shape trade and environmental policies. Ludema and Wooton (1994) show that strict environmental regulation replaces trade protection under free trade, since environmental policy has the same protectionist effects as trade policy. Rauscher (1991b) found that capital-market liberalization tightens the environmental tax and reduces emissions in one country since capital moves to the second country. The environmental tax goes up in the second country as well, but emissions may rise. The following chapters will show how political-economic analysis contributes to the understanding of the environmental effects of trade.

4 Economic Integration and the Environment: A Perfect-competition Approach with Applications to NAFTA[1]

4.1 INTRODUCTION

This chapter investigates how environmental policy is affected by trade liberalization under perfect competition. Just as in Chapters 5 and 6, this question is considered in the context of a model of political optimization by policy makers, who choose policies to maximize political support, or to maximize probabilities of re-election. Policies are thus politically endogenous. In contrast to Chapters 5 and 6, a general-equilibrium approach of perfect competition is applied to focus on the general-equilibrium effects of inter-industry trade in an economy with two sectors of production. The focus is on the effects of environmental policy on the remuneration of the factors. In contrast, Chapters 5 and 6 consider the case of intra-industry competition, in which environmental policy affects output and prices of international oligopolists and a domestic monopolist, respectively.

It will be shown how these general-equilibrium effects drive the results: not only is dirty production affected by environmental policy, but clean production is affected as well. The underlying structure is a specific-factor model of international trade which is augmented by an additional factor of production, the environment. Capital is sector specific and earns the residuals after labor has been paid according to its marginal product. Trade policies affect capital rents in each sector differently as one sector gains from trade and the other loses. The same happens with environmental policy: tight environmental policy reduces the productivity of capital and labor in the dirty sector and drives labor in the clean sector, where the productivity of capital is enhanced. The clean sector competes with the dirty sector for the mobile factor of production, labor, and since the dirty sector is affected by pollution

---

[1]   This chapter is based on Bommer and Schulze (1994).

regulation, labor movements affect the clean sector as well. This set-up was chosen because the conflict of interest between different groups of workers and producers mirrors the results of empirical investigations. Magee (1980) found that lobbying for trade protection is undertaken along sectoral lines rather than along factor lines.[2]

This chapter follows the literature on competitive markets, as surveyed in Subsection 2.2.1 New is the political-economy approach, which makes environmental policy endogenous to trade policies. It is shown that, under certain conditions, trade liberalization can be associated with improved environmental quality since governments rely on policy instruments at their disposal to make compensating adjustments that cater to different special-interest groups, of whom environmentalists are one.

While the model is general in following the tradition of a political-economy approach to explaining policy behavior, the empirical results, presented in Section 4.3, are particularly consistent with the observed outcome of NAFTA, where environmental issues were entangled with trade liberalization issues, and trade liberalization occurred together with more stringent environmental quality standards in the US. This approach complements, but differs in focus from, previous analyses of the relationship between NAFTA and the environment. Grossman and Krueger (1993) studied how trade policy would affect environmental quality in the context of the consequences of NAFTA, and concluded on the basis of trade patterns and projected growth that the free-trade agreement would result in a deterioration of environmental quality in the US and an improvement in environmental quality in Mexico. In their analysis, however, environmental policy is not endogenously adjusted to reflect political support objectives of the government. This chapter shows that when political endogeneity of environmental and trade policy is introduced, the predicted deterioration of environmental quality in the US as a consequence of liberalized trade does not occur.

4.2 THE MODEL

4.2.1 The Economic Sector

This chapter analyzes the impact of trade integration and endogenous environmental policy in the framework of a simple two-sector specific factors model as studied by Jones (1971), which is amended by

---

2   Some approaches which are based on common interests along factor lines and modeled in a Heckscher–Ohlin framework, are surveyed in Subsection 2.2.

environmental aspects. Consider two sectors, both of which are producing a tradable good with the help of sector-specific capital and labor, which is mobile between sectors. These assumptions on factor mobility seem restrictive; however, since political decisions are motivated by short-term considerations and installed capital can be reallocated between sectors only by very time-consuming investment–deinvestment processes, the assumption of sector specificity seems justified. Furthermore, workers are hired or made redundant much more easily when sectors expand or contract.[3] Production functions $f^i(K^i, L^i), i = I, II$ are assumed to have the standard neoclassical properties, and factor markets are assumed to be competitive so that factors are remunerated with their value marginal product. (*L* stands for labor, *K* for sector-specific capital, superscripts indicate the sectors.)

One sector may rely on the environment as additional input to its production process; in reality it is the sector which consumes the environment *relatively more*. It could be either sector in principle; at this stage it is assumed to be the US export sector. This is in accordance with earlier results showing that the industrial countries' export sectors tend to be more polluting (for example, Hillman and Bullard, 1978; Anderson, 1993), which will be discussed in greater detail in Section 4.3, where NAFTA is investigated empirically. We do not specify here the use of the environment since it takes a variety of forms such as the right to emit pollutants within specified limits in the production process, and the use of natural resources (water, woods) for industrial purposes. What matters is that this use produces negative externalities and can be restricted by environmental standards set by a regulating body, that is, the government. Hence the sectoral outputs are given by

$$x^I = g(V) \, f^I(K^I, L^I) \quad \text{and} \quad x^{II} = f^{II}(K^{II}, L^{II}) \qquad (4.1)$$

where x denotes the output of the respective sectors and $f_K, f_L > 0, f_{KK}, f_{LL} < 0$. (Subscripts of functions refer to partial derivatives.) The use of the environment (V) increases the individual firm's productivity at a diminishing rate. If the environment is not exploited at all, the term $g(V)$ vanishes: $g(0) = 1$. The set-up contains the standard specific factors model as a boundary case. Hence, $g(V)$ has these properties:

---

3   If workers are imperfectly mobile between sectors, they have a special interest in policies that foster the sector they are employed in. See Mussa (1982) for an analysis of this phenomenon. The same is true for highly specialized labor, which is regarded as human-capital specific to the respective sector. These specific employees side with the capitalists of their sector.

$g_v > 0, g_{vv} < 0$.[4] The import-competing good serves as numeraire, q denotes the relative price of the export good. The maximization problem of the economy's production sector as a whole can now be formulated as follows:

$$\max_{L^I,L^{II},V} \left[\begin{array}{l} q\ x^I + x^{II}\,;\ x^I = g(V)\ f^I\ (K^I, L^I), \\ x^{II} = f^{II}\ (K^{II}, L^{II}), V \leq \overline{V}, \overline{L} = L^I + L^{II} \end{array} \right], \qquad (4.2)$$

where $\overline{L}$ stands for the economy's total labor force, $\overline{V}$ gives the maximum use of the environment per period of time. For now, pollution is regarded as exogenously set by the government; the next section will endogenize it as a result of a political optimization process. Quantitative restrictions rather than taxes are modeled, because they are much more prevalent in real life for political-economic reasons (see Buchanan and Tullock, 1975). The maximization yields the following standard relations:

$$q\ g(V)f_L^I = f_L^{II} = w \qquad (4.3)$$

$$d\ L^I = -d\ L^{II} \qquad (4.4)$$

$$V = \overline{V}, \qquad (4.5)$$

where w denotes the wage rate, which is equalized across sectors as a consequence of labor mobility. The polluting industry will always utilize the environment to the maximum amount possible; therefore the distinction between V and $\overline{V}$ is dropped in the subsequent analysis. Capital owners of a

---

4   The production function is modeled multiplicatively separable for this reason: environmental protection forces a firm to allocate a certain amount of capital *and* labor toward these ends, thereby making both factors less productive in the production of x^I. In other words, the higher V, the more productive L^I *and* K^I. The complaints of employers as well as of workers that too harsh environmental standards will jeopardize employment point in this direction.

   Environmental regulation is modeled as limits on total environmental pollution (V) rather than as pollution standards. In reality both restrictions prevail. The 1990 Clean Air Act Amendments, for instance, contain both kinds of regulations. These Amendments tightened emission standards to reduce tailpipe emissions of automobiles and trucks. Limits to total environmental pollution were introduced under the Acid Deposition Control program, regulating sulfur dioxide emissions of power plants. Moreover, limits to total environmental pollution are used in the phase-out of ozone-depleting chemicals, in the lead-trading program and under 'bubbles' and 'offsets'. The type of restriction used determines the environmentalists' stand toward trade liberalization, as shown later on in this chapter. The choice of regulation is motivated by the strive for simplicity; however, the result has integrity under the alternative form of environmental control.

specific sector are residual claimants to the output. Their remuneration (Π^i) is given by

$$\Pi^I = q x^I - w L^I \quad = \tag{4.6}$$

$$q g(V)\left[f^I(L^I,K^I) - f_L^I(L^I,K^I)L^I\right]$$

$$\Pi^{II} = x^{II} - w L^{II} \quad = \quad f^{II}(L^{II},K^{II}) - f_L^{II}(L^{II},K^{II})L^{II}. \tag{4.7}$$

In order to derive the regulator's optimal policy and changes thereof, we first investigate how the economy (as opposed to the political sphere) reacts to an alteration, say an increase in the environmental use, that is, reduced environmental standards. Production in the polluting sector becomes more rewarding and therefore labor will be attracted to this sector. Output and profits will increase whereas they will decline in the second sector.[5] The reallocation of labor can be shown by totally differentiating (4.3)

$$g_V f_L^I \cdot q dV + q g(V) \cdot f_{LL}^I dL^I - f_{LL}^{II} dL^{II} = 0. \tag{4.8}$$

Substituting (4.4) into (4.8) gives

$$g_V f_L^I \cdot q dV + q g(V) \cdot f_{LL}^I dL^I + f_{LL}^{II} dL^I = 0 \tag{4.9}$$

and solving (4.9) with respect to dL^I / dV:

$$\frac{d L^I}{dV} = -\frac{g_V q f_L^I}{q g(V) f_{LL}^I + f_{LL}^{II}} \quad > 0. \tag{4.10}$$

The variation of profits can be shown by totally differentiating (4.6) and (4.7) with respect to L and V

$$d\Pi^I = q \cdot \begin{bmatrix} g_V(f(L^I,K^I) - f_L(L^I,K^I)L^I)dV \\ -(g(V) \cdot L^I \cdot f_{LL}^I(L^I,K^I))dL^I \end{bmatrix} \tag{4.11}$$

and

---

5   These effects are in spirit those of the Rybczynski theorem: an increase in one factor of production (here: V) raises the production of the sector that uses this factor relatively intensively (here: the export sector).

$$d\,\Pi^{II} = -f_{LL}^{II}\,L^{II}\,dL\,.$$
(4.12)

Solving (4.11) and (4.12) with respect to $d\Pi^I/dV$ and $d\Pi^{II}/dV$ yields:

$$\Pi_V^I = q\left[g_V(f^I - f_L^I\,L^I) - g(V)L^I\,f_{LL}^I\,\frac{d\,L^I}{d\,V}\right] > 0$$
(4.13)

$$\Pi_V^{II} = -L^{II}\,f_{LL}^{II}\,\frac{d\,L^{II}}{d\,V} = L^{II}\,f_{LL}^{II}\,\frac{d\,L^I}{d\,V} < 0.$$
(4.14)

The increase in pollution leaves the capitalists of the export sector better off while the import sector's capital owners are on the losing end. Labor profits from pollution. From equation (4.3) it follows that

$$w_V = f_{LL}^{II}\,\frac{d\,L^{II}}{d\,V} < 0.$$
(4.15)

Substituting (4.4) into (4.15) gives

$$w_V = -f_{LL}^{II}\,\frac{d\,L^I}{d\,V} > 0\,.$$
(4.16)

Obviously, there are conflicting interests among the three producer groups with regard to the level of environmental use. The capital owners of the clean sector favor tight regulation because regulation attracts labor, makes capital more productive and can therefore improve their profits. Labor and the capital owners of the dirty sector favor lenient regulation. Tight regulation decreases the wage rate and the profits of the dirty sector. Regulation reduces the productivity of labor because less of the complementary factor of production, the environment, is available. At the same time, labor leaves the dirty sector and decreases capital productivity in this sector as well. Since it is observed that there are environmental standards, the question arises how they are determined in the political process, which is characterized by opposing lobbying. This will be investigated in the next section.

4.2.2 A Simple Model of Environmental Regulation

As has been seen in the previous subsection, environmental regulation has three effects. First, it affects productivity (in the polluting sector) and hence the national product; second, it reallocates labor and redistributes income;

and this determines, third, the amount of negative externalities. These different effects cause individuals to have different interests with respect to the tightness of environmental standards – according to their capital ownership, preference (for a clean environment), and the degree to which they are affected by pollution. The regulating body setting the environmental standards consists of politicians who seek to maximize political support via their environmental policy.[6] Following Stigler's (1971) and Peltzman's (1976) theory of regulation, the study argues that the administration maximizes the following political support function:

$$M = M\left(\Pi^{I}, \Pi^{II}, \tilde{w}, V\right),$$ (4.17)

which is assumed to be twice continuously differentiable. The two industries will increase their support for the administration since their profits rise ($M_{\Pi^{I}} > 0$, $M_{\Pi^{II}} > 0$), workers support the administration in order to maximize their real wage $\tilde{w}$: $M_{\tilde{w}} > 0$. Since prices are held fixed for the moment, the real wage moves along with the nominal wage w, so that (4.16) applies. Lastly, the environmentalists trade their support against the improvement of the environment as such; consequently their utility (U) is strictly decreasing in V. Therefore $M_{U} > 0$ and $U_{V} < 0$. Furthermore the utility of the environmentalists decreases exponentially when pollution increases: $U_{VV} < 0$. This reflects standard assumptions made in environmental economics that damage increases exponentially as pollution expands. Diminishing marginal support or increasing marginal opposition, respectively, are assumed. Furthermore, individuals are assumed to be purely self-interested. Consequently, the political support function has the following additional properties: $M_{\Pi^{I}\Pi^{I}}, M_{\Pi^{II}\Pi^{II}}, M_{\tilde{w}\tilde{w}}, M_{UU} < 0$ and $M_{ij} = 0; \forall\, i \neq j$, $i, j = \Pi^{I}, \Pi^{II}, w, U$.

The support may take on various forms which may differ between the interest groups; for example, industries may find campaign contributions most effective whereas environmentalists may recommend the general public to cast their vote in a specified way. Our model is broad enough to encompass all these channels of exerting influence on the administration. The administration is maximizing its political support by equating support for a reduction and for an increase of environmental use at the margin, that is,

---

6   This chapter does not go into institutional details here, but notes instead that general principles of environmental regulation are typically laid down in federal laws (for example, the Clean Air Act) and are detailed and executed by the bureaucracy, such as the Environmental Protection Agency which is headed by a person appointed by the President. It is thus clear that decision makers are not independent experts, but politicians or people dependent on politicians, who maximize political support.

$$M_V = M_{\Pi'} \Pi_V^I + M_{\Pi''} \Pi_V^{II} + M_{\tilde{w}} \tilde{w}_V + M_V' = 0 \qquad (4.18)$$

This political equilibrium is unique as follows from the above assumption that the support function is concave in its arguments. It is dependent on the overall economic conditions; once the constraints alter, the politically optimal regulation will do the same. Peltzman (1976) has shown this for cost and demand shifts faced by a monopolist, and Hillman (1982) for trade protection of declining industries facing exogenous price shifts. In the next subsection, we analyze the effects of a changing constraint for the case of a trade liberalization understanding, since the removal of trade barriers is at the core of NAFTA.

4.2.3 Environmental Regulation and Trade Liberalization

Trade liberalization will alter the relative price of the export good and thereby incomes. The abolition of import barriers will make imports cheaper domestically. If the importing country is large, this removal of trade impediments will also increase the world price for the respective imports and thus raise the export prices of the country's trading partner. At any rate, the relative price of exports will increase.[7] This will make the export sector better off – again it attracts labor from the import sector, which will find its profits squeezed. These are standard results which are reported for the sake of completeness. Again the differentiation of equation (4.3) provides the reallocation of labor:

$$g(V)f_L^I \cdot dq + qg(V) \cdot f_{LL}^I dL^I - f_{LL}^{II} dL^{II} = 0 . \qquad (4.19)$$

Substituting (4.4) into (4.19) gives

$$g(V)f_L^I \cdot dq + qg(V) \cdot f_{LL}^I dL^I + f_{LL}^{II} dL^I = 0 \qquad (4.20)$$

and solving (4.20) with respect to dL^I/dV:

$$\frac{dL^I}{dq} = -\frac{g(V)f_L^I}{qg(V)f_{LL}^I + f_{LL}^{II}} > 0. \qquad (4.21)$$

---

7   In a multi-commodity world this is only true 'on average', but not for each single export and import commodity.

The variation of profits can be shown by totally differentiating (4.6) and (4.7) with respect to L and q :

$$d\Pi^I = g(V) \cdot \left[f(L^I, K^I) - f_L(L^I, K^I)L^I \right] dq$$
$$- \left[q \cdot g(V) \cdot L^I \cdot f_{LL}^I(L^I, K^I) \right] dL^I \tag{4.22}$$

and

$$d\Pi^{II} = -f_{LL}^{II} L^{II} dL . \tag{4.23}$$

Solving (4.22) and (4.23) with respect to $d\Pi^I/dq$ and $d\Pi^{II}/dq$ yields:

$$\Pi_q^I = g(V) \left(f^I - f_L^I L^I \right) - q\, g(V) L^I f_{LL}^I \frac{dL^I}{dq} > 0 \tag{4.24}$$

$$\Pi_q^{II} = f_{LL}^{II} \frac{dL^I}{dq} < 0 . \tag{4.25}$$

Trade liberalization increases the profits of sector one as sector one's relative price rises. Sector two's profits decline as reduced protection lowers its price.

The wage rate rises in terms of the import good, but decreases in terms of the export good so that labor's position remains ambiguous. However, Ruffin and Jones (1977) have shown that protection presumably hurts labor and thus workers should favor trade liberalization. The reason for this presumption is that the protected import good is in excess demand and that if the workers' consumption pattern is similar to the one of the economy as a whole the effect of more expensive exportables will be more than offset by cheaper import goods. Thus, it is assumed that $\tilde{w}_q > 0$.

We do not analyze the rationale for trade liberalization as explained in Chapter 1; this inquiry is concerned about how environmental policy is changed in the process of trade liberalization in order to restore a political support-maximizing equilibrium. This approach is focused directly on the case of the NAFTA negotiations, where the environmental parts of the agreement were added after trade liberalization principles had been agreed upon.

Note at the outset that trade liberalization has the same distributional impact as increased environmental use, since the US export sector is the pollution-intensive one. The optimal environmental standards will shift according to equation (4.18), which is differentiated with respect to q

$$\frac{dV}{dq} = -\frac{M_{Vq}}{M_{VV}}.$$ (4.26)

Consider M_{VV} first:

$$M_{VV} = M_{\Pi^I \Pi^I}\left(\Pi_V^I\right)^2 + M_{\Pi^I}\Pi_{VV}^I + M_{\Pi^{II}\Pi^{II}}\left(\Pi_V^{II}\right)^2$$
$$+ M_{\Pi^{II}}\Pi_{VV}^{II} + M_{\widetilde{w}\widetilde{w}}w_V^2 + M_{\widetilde{w}}w_{VV} + M'_{VV}$$ (4.27)

Recalling the assumption of positive and diminishing marginal support from the gainers from relaxed environmental regulation (workers, exporters) and increasing opposition from the pro-environment preservation interests (importers, 'true' environmentalists), equation (4.27) has a minus sign.[8] Obviously, this is the second-order condition for the existence of a political equilibrium, that is, an interior maximum of the political support function. Since it is observed that environmental pollution is restricted in real life this provides a second justification for M_{VV} to be negative

$$M_{Vq} = \underbrace{M_{\Pi^I \Pi^I}\Pi_q^I \Pi_V^I}_{<0} + \underbrace{M_{\Pi^I}}_{>0}\underbrace{\Pi_{Vq}^I}_{?} + \underbrace{M_{\Pi^{II}\Pi^{II}}\Pi_q^{II}\Pi_V^{II}}_{<0}$$
$$+ \underbrace{M_{\Pi^{II}}}_{>0}\underbrace{\Pi_{Vq}^{II}}_{?} + \underbrace{M_{\widetilde{w}\widetilde{w}}\widetilde{w}_q\widetilde{w}_V}_{<0} + \underbrace{M_{\widetilde{w}}}_{>0}\underbrace{\widetilde{w}_{Vq}}_{} + \underbrace{M'_{Vq}}_{\leq 0}.$$ (4.28)

Environmentalists are interested only in environmental quality. Since environmental control is modeled as a restriction on *total* environmental pollution (V), trade liberalization does not affect the environment – the restriction on V is unaltered. Thus, $U_q = U_{Vq} = 0$. If restrictions on pollution *per unit of output* were to be considered instead (see below) environmentalists would oppose trade liberalization, because the increased output of the (dirty) export sector would cause increased pollution. By the same token, concavity of the political support and profit functions are sufficient to signify equation (4.28) with a minus sign. This parallels the result on equation (4.27), which is not surprising since in this set-up an increase in the relative price of the export good works in the same direction as an increase of the environmental pollution by the export sector.

Hence, equation (4.26) will be negative. Note that respectively w_V and $\widetilde{w}_V$, or w_{VV} and $\widetilde{w}_{VV}$, are identical up to a scaling factor. The

---

8   The sufficient assumption is that the political support function and the profit functions are concave in q and V. Environmentalists' utility function exhibits the standard properties.

environmental standards will become more restrictive as a consequence of the removal of trade barriers. Trade liberalization is beneficial to the polluting export sector and labor, but hurts the clean import sector. In order to re-establish a political support-maximizing equilibrium, the government will trade off some of this gain to the suffering second sector by tightening up the environmental control. This reduces the scope of income redistribution and the reallocation of labor, and additionally ensures the regulator increased political support by the environmentalists. It is the windfall gain for the exporting sector and labor from liberalization that makes the shift in environmental policy possible. At the same time it makes this shift necessary. In order to re-equate marginal political support, the government must reallocate some of the gains accruing to a specific group to the other groups involved since the marginal political support is decreasing. Environmental policy and trade policy are substitutive tools for income redistribution, but at the same time they have a different substitution relationship for environmentalists who are interested in the environment as such.

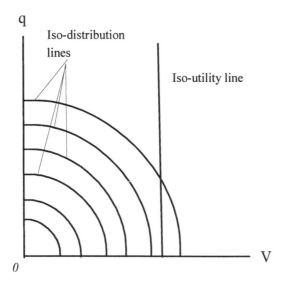

Figure 4.1:   Iso-distribution lines if the export sector is polluting

This is demonstrated with the help of Figure 4.1, which depicts the iso-distribution lines[9] for the case that the export sector is polluting. This is what

9   To be precise, not only the income *distribution* remains constant on these lines, but also the absolute income of each individual group.

was assumed. Totally differentiating equation (4.3) shows that there are combinations of trade policies (q) and environmental policies (V), which hold the wage rate constant:

$$dw = q \cdot g_V f_L^I dV + g(V) \cdot f_L^I dq = 0. \qquad (4.29)$$

Solving (4.29) with respect to dq/dV yields:

$$\frac{dq}{dV} = -\frac{q\, g_V}{g(V)} \quad < 0. \qquad (4.30)$$

It is straightforward to show that not only the wage rate, but also the profits are unchanged if equation (4.30) holds. Totally differentiating equation (4.6) with respect to the profits of sector one, setting it at zero and solving it with respect to dq/dV also yields equation (4.30). Since a change in trade and environmental policies keeps the wage rate constant, labor allocation stays constant as well. Hence, if no labor moves between the sectors, capital productivity stays constant and profits are unchanged.

Regulators availing themselves of trade protection and environmental policies can choose any point on the concave locus without affecting the political support of the producer lobbies. However, environmentalist support decreases at increasing rates as they move down the line, because of deteriorating environmental quality. With environmental control taking the form of restrictions on total pollution (V), the environmentalists' indifference curve is vertical.

If pollution is limited per unit of output, results do not change. To see this, let v denote the maximum pollution per unit of output. Then, environmental pollution V is given by equation (4.31)

$$V = v x^I = v\, g(v)\, f^I(K^I, L^I). \qquad (4.31)$$

Other things being equal, trade liberalization causes a deterioration in the environment, as can be seen if differentiating (4.31) with respect to q:

$$dV/dq = v\, g(v) f_L^I\, dL^I/dq > 0. \qquad (4.32)$$

Hence, the utility of the environmentalists decreases when trade is liberalized: $U_q = U_v V_q < 0$. This modification does not alter the basic result. If pollution is limited per unit of output (to v) and this instrument is depicted on the abscissa, the indifference curve slopes downward and will still be steeper than the iso-distribution line. The indifference curve will have to satisfy $dV = 0$. Totally differentiating (4.31) gives:

$$dV = [\,g(v)f^I(K^I, L^I) + vg_v f^I(K^I, L^I) + vg(v)f_L^I \tfrac{dL^I}{dv}\,]\,dv$$
$$+ vg(v)f_L^I \tfrac{dL^I}{dq}\,dq = 0. \tag{4.33}$$

Substituting (4.10) and (4.21) into (4.33) and solving it with respect to dq/dV yields the slope of the indifference curve of the environmentalists:

$$\left.\frac{dq}{dv}\right|_{dV=0} = \frac{f^I(g+v\,g_v)\,[qgf_{LL}^I + f_{LL}^{II}]}{v\,g^2\,(f_L^I)^2} - \frac{q\,g_v}{g} < 0. \tag{4.34}$$

Comparing (4.34), the slope of the indifference curve, with equation (4.30), the slope of the iso-distribution line of the non-environmental interests, equation (4.35) illustrates the following:

$$\left.\frac{dq}{dv}\right|_{dV=0} = \frac{f^I\Big(g+v\,g_v\Big)\Big(qgf_{LL}^I + f_{LL}^{II}\Big)}{v\,g^2\,(f_L^I)^2} - \frac{q\,g_v}{g}$$
$$< -\frac{q\,g_v}{g} = \left.\frac{dq}{dv}\right|_{d\Pi^I = d\Pi^{II} = 0}. \tag{4.35}$$

The indifference curve is steeper than the iso-distribution line. It is thus clear that the argument holds likewise if the environmental policy tools are ceilings on pollution per output rather than on total pollution.

Since political support is derived from producer lobbies only interested in their income, and from environmentalists only caring about V, the iso-support line must lie between the iso-distribution line and the environmentalists' vertical indifference curve. The iso-support locus is a weighted combination of these two graphs with the environmentalists' relative weight decreasing for decreasing V (diminishing marginal support). This makes it clear that the concave iso-*support* lines must have a steeper slope than the iso-*distribution* lines. It also directly implies that all groups are affected by an iso-support variation. Figure 4.2 illustrates this. The solid line represents the iso-distribution locus that runs through the initial pre-liberalization point I, characterized by the relative export price q^1 and the level of environmental regulation V^1. The vertical indifference curve of the environmentalists in the initial situation is depicted by the longer-dashes line and, consequently, the associated iso-support line is given by the shorter-dashes line. These results have three important implications.

First, a variation of q and V that leaves the political support unchanged will trade off a reduction of tariffs against an increase in environmental protection. This is what was observed in the case of NAFTA, which was the first international agreement on trade liberalization to incorporate environmental support measures explicitly. Graphically this simultaneous variation of trade and environmental policy is represented by the movement from the initial point I to point B along the iso-support line: q^2 marks the relative export price under free trade and V^2 gives the associated level of environmental regulation that keeps political support constant.

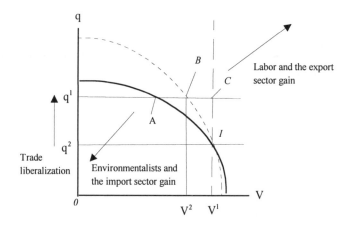

*Figure 4.2:   Gainers and losers from trade liberalization cum
                 environmental policy tightening*

Second, such a variation will not leave the income distribution unchanged. The income redistribution due to the elimination of tariffs is only partly offset by a redistribution owing to increased environmental control. In the new political equilibrium (point B) the export sector and labor obtain a net gain because their profits are higher at B than at point A on the iso-distribution curve while the import sector loses. Because of diminishing marginal political support (or increasingly rising opposition) the sum of producers' political support declines: the import sector reduces its support by more than the exporters and workers increase theirs. This net reduction is offset by an increased support from environmentalists since pollution has been reduced.

Third, environmental quality is improved! This is obvious in the case of restrictions on total pollution (V) analyzed here; environmental pollution is reduced from V^1 to V^2 (shift from point I to point B) as the pollution limits are reduced accordingly. This general result also holds if standards (pollution limits per unit of output) are the chosen instrument. In that case, the indifference curve is also downward sloping and still steeper than the iso-distribution line, with the iso-support line lying between them. This was shown with equation (4.35) and implies that point C on the indifference curve, denoting equal environmental quality as in the initial state, is still to the right of point B.[10] The support-maximizing tightening of environmental standards in the course of trade liberalization more than offsets the structural shift toward the pollution-intensive export sectors. In both cases, the environmentalists stand to gain and so does the environment.

We assumed the export sector to be more pollution intensive. There are two reasons in favor of this assumption: first, the empirical evidence on actual pollution of the respective sectors (dealt with in Section 4.3) and, second, the predicted policy reaction of environmental policy to trade liberalization, which depends on the assumption of the relative pollution intensity of the sectors. To see this, assume now, contrary to the assumptions, that the import sector is the polluting one. In that case equation (4.3) would become:

$$q \, g(V) f_L^I = f_L^{II} = w. \tag{4.3*}$$

Consequently, the iso-income lines would have to satisfy the following property:

$$\frac{dq}{dV} = \frac{g_V \, f_L^{II}}{f_L^I} \quad > 0 \tag{4.20*}$$

and would look as depicted in Figure 4.3 A political support-maximizing incumbent would trade off a reduction of trade protection against a reduction in environmental protection. That is exactly what is not observed in the US! This result lends support to the assumption that the export sector's production is environment intensive. But there is more corroborating evidence than that, and this will be investigated in the next section.

---

10   In the case of standards, the corresponding figure would be drawn in the (v, q) plane.

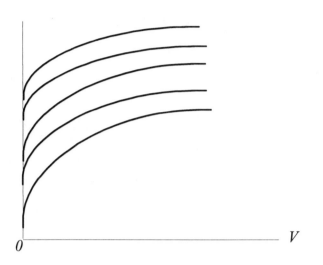

Figure 4.3:   Iso-distribution lines if the import sector is polluting

One might be tempted to conclude – following this symmetrical argument – that NAFTA causes a deterioration in the Mexican environment. However, in contrast to the US, NAFTA provides a substantial growth stimulus for the Mexican economy (see Brown et al., 1992a) which makes the case non-symmetrical. In addition there have been indications of efforts by the US government to induce its Mexican counterpart to enhance its environmental control. Since such growth effects have, besides composition effects, a major impact on the Mexican environment, an analysis of the effects of NAFTA on the Mexican environment needs to consider both effects.[11]

---

11 Grossman and Krueger (1993) anticipate such positive growth effects for Mexico which are based on the environmental Kuznets curve (see Section 3). They estimate that emissions of SO_2 and particulates increase until a per-capita income of $4000–5000 is reached, and fall thereafter. With a current per-capita income of $5000 Mexico is at the peak of these emissions. Hence, NAFTA-induced growth could contribute to a decline of emissions. However, for some types of pollutants, for example, CO_2, emissions increase further with higher-income levels.

4.3   NAFTA, SECTORAL CHANGE AND THE ENVIRONMENT

The previous section has shown that environmental policy will be tightened in the process of trade liberalization if the export sector is relatively dirtier, but will be relaxed if the import-competing sector is relatively dirtier. This section investigates empirically which case applies to the US under NAFTA.

Trade liberalization creates winners and losers, depending on the composition of trade and removed protection: some sectors will expand at the expense of others. This structural shift affects pollution, since sectors pollute to a different extent. Hence, the focus is on the composition effects of NAFTA,[12] and we proceed in three steps. First, estimated changes in composition for the US are borrowed from existing computable general-equilibrium (CGE) models and, second, pollution intensities for the various sectors are derived from toxic release data. Third, by combining both data sets, the environmental impact of the sectoral changes is calculated. This empirical approach, which assumes constant environmental control, serves to justify the assumptions in the model regarding the pollution intensity of the two sectors; it is not the description of the real changes in environmental quality because environmental policy is endogenous. Trade liberalization will have sizable sectoral effects although the US average tariff for Mexican goods is moderate (only 3.4 percent), because tariffs vary considerably between sectors (see Weintraub, 1992a, 1992b). Brown, Deardorff and Stern (1992a, henceforth BDS) analyze sectoral shifts in a CGE model, assuming the complete elimination of tariffs between the US, Canada and Mexico, as well as a 25 percent reduction on import quota on agricultural products, food, textiles and apparel from Mexico.[13] They find overall effects are not overly large, but significant sectoral shifts are sizable: US exports are expected to increase for clothing (10 percent), footwear (11.2 percent), furniture (9.8 percent), rubber products (6.2 percent), chemicals (3.7 percent) and iron and steel (6.5 percent), to list only a few; US imports will increase in glass (57.6 percent), electrical machinery (10.0 percent), non-ferrous metals (5.3 percent) and furniture and fixtures (3.6 percent), among others.

Next, the relative environmental burden of US exports compared to US imports and its change due to NAFTA are analyzed (for details see Tables

---

12   Other factors influencing environmental conditions, such as growth effects of NAFTA, seem to be very small, looking at the size of the US economy compared to the Mexican economy. Brown et al. (1992a) find only a 0.1 percent increase in GDP for the US economy.

13   In another scenario, BDS assume a 10 percent increase in the capital stock of the Mexican economy. Although investment liberalization is a big issue in NAFTA, this study confines itself to analyzing the effects of trade liberalization because the effects of investment liberalization are highly uncertain at the moment.

4A.1–4). The environment will deteriorate *ceteris paribus* if the estimated increase in US exports is relatively dirtier than the expected import changes. Toxic release data of the manufacturing sectors are used as an indicator for industrial pollution levels and they are combined with actual sectoral export and import data, as well as with the data of expected sectoral export and import changes under NAFTA as computed by BDS.[14]

The toxic release per unit of export production turns out to be considerably higher (by 37 percent) than the pollution generated by the production of the import goods (Table 4A.1). Toxic release of export production was estimated to be 1.5 pounds/$1000 compared to only 1.1 pounds/$1000 of toxic release in import production. The toxic release content of *expected trade changes* is even more dramatic: the production of expected changes of exports causes the release of 1.9 pounds/$1000 compared with only 0.7 pounds/$1000 for import changes, that is, the expected export changes are no less than two and a half times dirtier than the imports. To demonstrate the robustness of the results, another CGE model was applied, the KPMG Peat Marwick Model, analyzing the US–Mexico trade changes under NAFTA and similar results are obtained (Table 4A.2).[15] Toxic release of export production was estimated to be 1.5 pounds/$1000 compared to only 1.1 pounds/$1000 of toxic release in import production. The toxic release of expected changes of exports causes the release of 1.3 pounds/$1000 compared to only 0.9 pounds/$1000 for import changes. Our calculations show clearly that the US specializes in the export of dirty products, which is further increased as a result of NAFTA.

In addition, the robustness of the results is checked by using pollution abatement and control expenditures (PACE), a different concept of measuring the pollution impact of industries. A shortcoming of PACE is that they do not measure pollution directly, as toxic release data do, but they measure clean-up expenses of the various industries (see Appendix 2A). Hence, this measure is for this purpose less valuable. The results obtained by PACE are less clear-cut than the toxic release results, but they still point in the same direction: US export production is more pollution intensive than import production. For trade data from BDS, the PACE of exports and imports is not significantly different: exports contain 0.47 percent of PACE and imports contain 0.46 percent (see Table 4A.3). Only the expected export changes contain higher PACE (0.49 percent of output) than expected import changes do (0.44 percent of output). Applying the KPMG Peat Marwick Model, analyzing the US–Mexico trade changes under NAFTA, again results are not very clear-cut. US exports to Mexico contain 0.51 percent of PACE and are 'dirtier' than import production, which contains 0.46 percent of

14 The concept of toxic release data is explained in Appendix 2A.
15 The KPMG Peat Marwick model is reported in Hufbauer and Schott (1992, pp. 66–8).

PACE (see Table 4A.4). Expected changes in exports to Mexico contain 0.45 percent of PACE and are again slightly dirtier than expected changes in imports which contain 0.43 percent of PACE. Table 4.1 gives an overview of the results.

Table 4.1: Summary of the pollution intensity results of US manufacturing

Pollution intensity of	BDS data pounds of toxic release/ $1000 output	KPMG data pounds of toxic release/ $1000 output	BDS data PACE in percent of output	KPMG data PACE in percent of output
Exports	1.5	1.5	0.47	0.51
Imports	1.1	1.1	0.46	0.46
Expected export changes	1.9	1.3	0.49	0.45
Expected import changes	0.7	0.9	0.44	0.43

The results are in line with the existing body of literature on the environmental effects of trade liberalization. Anderson (1993) provides evidence for the effects of trade liberalization on the environment in general. He finds that developing countries protect their import-competing and often dirty heavy industries, while discouraging their primary and labor-intensive sectors. On the other hand, industrial countries often protect labor intensive sectors such as textiles and agriculture. Trade liberalization will shift production to the sectors with comparative advantage: poor countries will probably get relief from environmental pressure by specializing in labor-intensive and relatively clean production whereas industrial countries will tend to specialize in dirty industries. Lucas et al. (1992) provide corroborating evidence (compare Chapter 3). In a study on developing countries, they find by measuring sectoral toxic releases that open economies tend to have an industrial structure that is less polluting than the structure of closed economies. The opening-up will therefore cause a sectoral change in production from smokestack industries to cleaner ones. Again, liberalizing trade in developing countries will shift dirty production to the countries of comparative advantage: the industrial countries.[16]

---

16 Subsection 2.2.3 provides evidence from other empirical studies regarding the pollution content of US trade. In contrast to the approach chosen here, which examines current and possible future pollution impacts of trade, these studies examine the pollution content for past decades.

These general results carry over to the case of NAFTA – dirty production will tend to shift to the US, increasing pollution there. Grossman and Krueger (1993) interpret the expected shift of utility output (including electricity) from Mexico to the US, as predicted by the BDS model, as an indication that energy-intensive and therefore dirty production shifts to the US.[17] In a second approach, Grossman and Krueger combine estimated changes of sectoral output from the BDS model with toxic release data. They find the toxic release of Mexican industrial production to be reduced by 261 thousand pounds, whereas it increases considerably in the US (13,053 thousand pounds).

To sum up, there is considerable empirical evidence that NAFTA will cause the dirty US export sector to grow at the expense of the cleaner import sector, and would thereby – for a given environmental policy – cause the environmental balance of the US to deteriorate.[18] The assumptions on the relative pollution intensities are justified in the light of the empirical results presented. Our theoretical considerations, however, have shown that, with the export sector being the polluting one in the US, environmental policy is endogenously tightened. The losers of trade liberalization, that is, the clean import-competing sector, are partly compensated and the environmentalists are satisfied through higher environmental quality.

Reality confirms the results. NAFTA is the first trade agreement in history which explicitly includes environmental protection. Three points in the agreement make tightened environmental policy obvious (see Esty, 1994b and Thomas and Tereposky, 1993). First, there are various environmental provisions in the treaty itself. NAFTA members are allowed to use trade sanctions provided by international environmental agreements. Their justification is easier than under GATT. Environmental policy should avoid 'unnecessary obstacles to trade', which allows more scope than the GATT term 'least trade restrictive'. In a dispute settlement, the complaining country bears the burden of proof if it attacks the environmental policy of the other country as being trade restrictive. This is opposite to GATT rules. Second, the Environmental Side Agreement creates an institutional body for supervising environmental issues affected by trade liberalization. Third, the Integrated Environmental Border Plan develops cooperation between the environmental agencies of the US and Mexico. The Border Plan develops a

17 Electricity production is a major part of the utility sector. Since disaggregated data are not available, Grossman and Krueger project the utility output change to the change of electricity production.
18 One may surmise that a country with high environmental standards, like the US, specializes in clean production. However, the empirical studies, surveyed in Subsection 2.2.3, find that environmental regulation has no significant impact on trade patterns. Environmental control costs are negligible compared to other factor costs, such as wages, which are decisive in determining the pattern of comparative advantage.

Commission for Environmental Cooperation, a forum for the upward harmonization of environmental standards and provides a multi-billion dollar funding for loans to the private sector for environmental infrastructure projects and $1.8 billion of World Bank and Inter-American Development Bank loans. The Border XXI Environmental Program addresses infrastructure needs as well as forest and coastal conservation. A Binational Pollution Control Zone mitigates the border region's notoriously polluted air (see *International Environmental Reporter*, 1996a, 1996b). Additionally, governments have agreed upon spending on a large scale to further improve the environment.

4.4 CONCLUDING REMARKS

This chapter provides the first step in the political-economic analysis of economic integration and the environment; previous studies have neglected the endogenous character of environmental policy. We show that results change considerably when the political process that determines the degree of environmental control is taken into account.

There are studies indicating that the structural shift due to NAFTA will tend to increase pollution in the US; however, these do not take the endogenous character of environmental policy into account. This chapter has shown that the endogenous variation of environmental policy in the course of trade liberalization even reverses the impact of NAFTA on the environment. In order to re-establish a political support-maximizing equilibrium the administration trades off some of the gains from trade liberalization accruing to the export sector and to labor to the losers of removed protection, that is, the owners of factors specific to the import sector. This is affected through a tightened environmental control, which tends to place the dirty export sector and labor at a disadvantage and fosters the clean import sector. In doing so the administration increases its political support from the environmentalists. Trade policy and environmental policy turn out to be substitutive tools for distributional purposes; but because of the political influence of environmentalist groups, trade liberalization cum environmental policy tightening has distributional impacts on a net basis. Exporters gain, importers lose and the environment is improved.

Empirical results support the theoretical analysis. Ample evidence is presented that the US export sector is relatively more polluting. Moreover, the predicted environmental policy reaction in the course of trade liberalization is in line with reality: the agreement itself and its environmental side agreement provide indications that the administration is striving for increased environment protection. For example, the administration has bound itself to spend $1 billion on the Border Plan and to set up an Environmental Protection Commission to coordinate technical assistance (see Salinas-León, 1993, p. 30).

APPENDIX 4A: MEASURING THE POLLUTION INTENSITY OF US MANUFACTURING

Data Sources for Appendix Tables

Trade data are taken from the *Statistical Abstract of the US 1992*, CGE estimates on trade changes under NAFTA are obtained from Brown et al. (1992a) and from the study of KPMG Peat Marwick as reported by Hufbauer and Schott (1992, pp. 66–8). Production values were taken from the *Statistical Abstract of the US 1991* and the *Industry Statistics Yearbook 1990* of the UN. Toxic release data were provided by the *Toxic Release Inventories 1992–94* of the US Environmental Protection Agency. PACE data were taken from Low (1992b). Some sectors of production were reclassified to fit in the two-digit SIC listing.

Table 4A.1:   *Pollution intensity of US trade measured with toxic release data and with results obtained by a CGE study from Brown et al. (1992a)*

Code	SIC listing	US exports world $mil	Est. US exports in percent (BDS)
20, 21	food, kindred products	18,837	1.870
22	textile mill products	2,794	7.730
23	apparel and related products	2,349	10.010
24	lumber and related products	6,050	1.920
25	furniture and fixtures	1,011	9.800
26	paper and allied products	8,126	2.350
27	printing and publishing	2,598	1.700
28	chemicals and allied products	3,5825	3.730
29	petroleum and coal products	5,019	–0.050
30	rubber and miscellaneous plastics products	5,010	6.150
31	leather and leather products	1,131	1.160
32	stone, clay and glass products	2,638	4.830
33	iron, steel, nonferrous metals	5,419	2.800
34	fabricated metal products	9,117	6.020
35	machinery, excluding electrical	55,524	3.940
36	electric and electronic machinery	32,718	1.840
37	transportation equipment	56,875	–0.180
38, 39	miscellaneous manufactured commodities	21,880	4.050
	Total	272,921	
	Toxic release in pounds/$1000	1.49	

Increase exports $1000	US imports world in $mil	Est. US imports in percent (BDS)	Increase of imports $1000
352,252	15,210	1.710	260,091
215,976	7,294	0.230	16,776
235,135	22,841	1.470	335,763
116,160	5,848	0.860	50,293
99,078	5,148	3.580	184,298
190,961	11,880	0.090	10,692
44,166	1,807	0.170	3,072
1,336,272	20,118	−0.480	−96,566
−2,509	11,979	0.520	62,291
308,115	9,488	0.540	51,235
13,120	9,837	1.930	189,854
127,415	5,775	0.730	28,660
193,998	22,622	3.415	763,474
548,843	11,568	2.710	313,493
2,187,646	54,051	0.010	5,405
602,011	55,361	9.970	5,519,492
−102,375	87,972	2.130	1,873,804
886,140	35,208	−0.760	−267,581
7,352,404	394,007		9,304,545
1.87	1.10		0.73

Note: The values indicate the average of toxic release in pound per $1000 output weighted by sectoral trade data or expected changes, respectively.

Table 4A.1 Continued

Code	SIC listing	US sectoral output in $mil	Sectoral toxic release in pounds
20, 21	food, kindred products	390,200	38,520,898
22	textile mill products	67,300	31,901,256
23	apparel and related products	65,000	1,356,111
24	lumber and related products	70,000	35,064,103
25	furniture and fixtures	38,750	64,715,188
26	paper and allied products	131,400	256,465,577
27	printing and publishing	149,900	57,010,004
28	chemicals and allied products	278,100	2,080,313,266
29	petroleum and coal products	143,700	95,847,191
30	rubber and miscellaneous plastics products	98,400	183,531,840
31	leather and leather products	9,700	13,394,500
32	stone, clay and glass products	63,600	36,630,204
33	iron, steel, nonferrous metals	153,000	538,821,368
34	fabricated metal products	162,200	135,876,404
35	machinery, excluding electrical	253,600	57,362,647
36	electric and electronic machinery	192,300	99,793,767
37	transportation equipment	366,000	20,4957,096
38, 39	miscellaneous manufactured commodities	153,000	80,859,631
	Total	2,786,150	4,012,421,051

Toxic release pounds per $1000 of output	Toxic release of exports in pounds	Toxic release of US exports in pounds	Toxic release of imports in pounds	Toxic release of increase of US imp. in pounds
0.099	1,859,606	34,775	1,501,545	25,676
0.474	1,324,400	102,376	3,457,470	7,952
0.021	49,008	4,906	476,537	7,005
0.501	3,030,540	58,186	2,929,355	25,192
1.670	1,688,440	165,467	8,597,517	307,791
1.952	15,860,268	372,716	23,187,299	20,869
0.380	988,072	16,797	687,239	1,168
7.480	267,987,137	9,995,920	150491,702	−722,360
0.667	3,347,648	−1,674	7989,934	41,548
1.865	9,344,456	574,684	17,696,647	95,562
1.381	1,561,771	18,117	13,583,680	262,165
0.576	1,519,347	73,384	3,326,092	16,507
3.522	19,084,137	683,204	79,668,085	2,688,733
0.838	7,637,393	459,771	9,690,618	262,616
0.226	12,559,163	494,831	12,225,980	1,223
0.519	16,978,952	312,413	28,729,499	2,864,331
0.560	31,849,549	−57,329	49,263,622	1,049,315
0.528	11,563,456	468,320	18,607,228	−141,415
∅: 1.29	408,233,343	13,776,865	432110,049	6,813,878

Table 4A.2: Pollution intensity of US trade measured with toxic release data and with results obtained by a CGE study from KPMG

Code	SIC listing	US exports to Mexico 1988 in $1000	Expected change of US exports in $1000
20,21	food, kindred products	870,000	65,700
22	textile mill products	335,000	13,500
23	apparel and related products	242,000	30,000
24	lumber and related products	180,000	14,800
25	furniture and fixtures	125,000	−1,400
26	paper and allied products	733,000	13,600
27	printing and publishing	64,000	−0,500
28	chemicals and allied products	1,818,000	123,300
29	petroleum and coal products	319,000	15,700
30	rubber and miscellaneous plastics products	779,000	62,600
31	leather and leather products	68,000	1,100
32	stone, clay and glass products	184,000	5,900
33	iron, steel, nonferrous metals	866,000	25,900
34	fabricated metal products	703,000	57,000
35	machinery, excluding electrical	2,306,000	189,400
36	electric and electronic machinery	4,513,000	372,400
37	transportation equipment	2,030,000	142,500
38,39	miscellaneous manufactured commodities	988,000	89,000
	Total	17,123,000	1,220,500
	Toxic release in pounds/$1000	1.50	1.31

US imports from Mexico 1988 in $1000	Expected change of US imports in $1000
559,000	92,500
133,000	62,000
506,000	399,800
208,000	20,800
461,000	51,800
342,000	42,700
24,000	1,900
671,000	75,600
204,000	18,700
324,000	48,300
184,000	30,800
486,000	64,300
1,117,000	171,300
469,000	58,600
919,000	113,100
6,015,000	971,100
3,272,000	401,500
864,000	117,400
16,758,000	2,742,200
1.07	0.89

Table 4A.2 Continued

Code	SIC listing	US sectoral output in $mil	Sectoral toxic release in pounds
20, 21	food, kindred products	390,200	38,520,898
22	textile mill products	67,300	31,901,256
23	apparel and related products	65,000	1,356,111
24	lumber and related products	70,000	35,064,103
25	furniture and fixtures	38,750	64,715,188
26	paper and allied products	131,400	256,465,577
27	printing and publishing	149,900	57,010,004
28	chemicals and allied products	278,100	2,080,313,266
29	petroleum and coal products	143,700	95,847,191
30	rubber and miscellaneous plastics products	98,400	183,531,840
31	leather and leather products	9,700	13,394,500
32	stone, clay and glass products	63,600	36,630,204
33	iron, steel, nonferrous metals	153,000	538,821,368
34	fabricated metal products	162,200	135,876,404
35	machinery, excluding electrical	253,600	57,362,647
36	electric and electronic machinery	192,300	99,793,767
37	transportation equipment	366,000	204,957,096
38,39	miscellaneous manufactured commodities	153,000	80,859,631
	Total	2,786,150	4,012,421,051

Toxic release in pd. per $1000 output	Toxic release of exports in pounds	Toxic release of increase of US exports in pounds	Toxic release of imports in pounds	Toxic release of increase of US imports in pounds
0.099	85,887	6,486	55,185	9,132
0.474	158,795	6,399	63,044	29,389
0.021	5,049	0,626	10,557	8,341
0.501	90,165	7,414	104,190	10,419
1.670	208,759	−2,338	769,902	86,510
1.952	1430,664	26,544	667,513	83,342
0.380	24,340	−0,190	9,128	0,723
7.480	13,599,459	922,340	5,019,382	565,522
0.667	212,771	10,472	136,067	12,473
1.865	1,452,960	116,759	604,312	90,087
1.381	93,900	1,519	254,081	42,531
0.576	105,974	3,398	279,910	37,033
3.522	3,049,799	91,212	3,933,748	603,269
0.838	588,909	47,749	392,886	49,090
0.226	521,602	42,841	207,872	25,582
0.519	2,342,014	193,256	3,121,474	503,951
0.560	1,136,784	79,799	1,832,294	224,837
0.528	522,152	47,036	456,619	62,045
∅: 1.29	25,629,985	1,601,322	17,918,165	2,444,275

Table 4A.3:   *Pollution intensity of US trade measured with PACE data and*
              with results obtained by a CGE study by Brown et al. (1992a)

Code	SIC listing	US exports world $1000	Est. US exports in percent
20,21	food, kindred products	18,837,000	1.870
22	textile mill products	2,794,000	7.730
23	apparel and related products	2,349,000	10.010
24	lumber and related products	6,050,000	1.920
25	furniture and fixtures	1,011,000	9.800
26	paper and allied products	8,126,000	2.350
27	printing and publishing	2,598,000	1.700
28	chemicals and allied products	35,825,000	3.730
29	petroleum and coal products	5,019,000	−0.050
30	rubber and miscellaneous plastics products	5,010,000	6.150
31	leather and leather products	1,131,000	1.160
32	stone and clay	1,008,000	4.830
322	glass	1,129,000	−1.910
332	iron and steel	3,644,000	6.490
333	nonferrous metals	4,775,000	−0.890
34	fabricated metal products	9,117,000	6.020
35	machinery, excluding electrical	55,524,000	3.940
36	electric and electronic machinery	32,718,000	1.840
37	transportation equipment	56,875,000	−0.180
38,39	miscellaneous manufactured commodities	21,880,000	4.050
	Total	275,420,000	
	Average PACE in percent of output	0.47	

Note: The values indicate the average PACE weighted by sectoral trade data or expected changes, respectively.

Increase $1000	US imports world $1000	Estimated US imports percent
3,52,252	15,210,000	1,710
215,976	7,294,000	0,230
235,135	22,841,000	1,470
116,160	5,848,000	0,860
99,078	5,148,000	3,580
190,961	11,880,000	0,090
44,166	1,807,000	0,170
1,336,272	20,118,000	-0,480
−2,509	11,979,000	0,520
308,115	9,488,000	0,540
13,120	9,837,000	1,930
48,686	3,926,000	0,730
−21,564	1,770,000	57,640
236,496	11,549,000	1,510
−42,498	11,073,000	5,320
548,843	11,568,000	2,710
2,187,646	54,051,000	0,010
602,011	55,361,000	9,970
−102,375	87,972,000	2,130
886,140	35,208,000	-0,760
7,252,111	393,928,000	
0.49	0.46	

Table 4A.3 Continued

Code	SIC listing	Increase exports in $1000	PACE abatement cost in percent of output
20,21	food, kindred products	260,091	0.330
22	textile mill products	16,776	0.540
23	apparel and related products	335,763	0.540
24	lumber and related products	50,293	0.330
25	furniture and fixtures	184,298	0.300
26	paper and allied products	10,692	1.100
27	printing and publishing	3,072	0.140
28	chemicals and allied products	−96,566	1.180
29	petroleum and coal products	62,291	1.530
30	rubber and miscellaneous plastics products	51,235	0.300
31	leather and leather products	189,854	0.240
32	stone and clay	28,660	0.700
322	glass	1,020,228	0.700
332	iron and steel	174,390	1.120
333	nonferrous metals	589,084	1.120
34	fabricated metal products	313,493	0.480
35	machinery, excluding electrical	5,405	0.180
36	electric and electronic machinery	5,519,492	0.350
37	transportation equipment	1,873,804	0.280
38,39	miscellaneous manufactured commodities	−267,581	0.220
	Total	10,324,772	US industrial average
	Average PACE in percent of output	0.44	(0.54)

PACE in $1000 of exports	PACE in $1000 of increase US exports	PACE in $1000 of imports	PACE in $1000 of increase US imports
62,162	1,162	50,193	0,858
15,088	1,166	39,388	0,091
12,685	1,270	123,341	1,813
19,965	0,383	19,298	0,166
3,033	0,297	15,444	0,553
89,386	2,101	130,680	0,118
3,637	0,062	2,530	0,004
422,735	15,768	237,392	−1,139
76,791	−0,038	183,279	0,953
15,030	0,924	28,464	0,154
2,714	0,031	23,609	0,456
7,056	0,341	27,482	0,201
7,903	−0,151	12,390	7,142
40,813	2,649	129,349	1,953
53,480	−0,476	124,018	6,598
43,762	2,634	55,526	1,505
99,943	3,938	97,292	0,010
114,513	2,107	193,763	19,318
159,250	−0,287	246,322	5,247
48,136	1,950	77,458	−0,589
1,298,081	35,832	1,817,217	45,410

Table 4A.4:   Pollution intensity of US trade measured with PACE data and with results obtained by a CGE study from KPMG

Code	SIC listing	1988 US exports to Mexico in $1000	Expected change of US exports in $1000
206	sugar	17,000	−0,700
20	food	870,000	65,700
22	textiles	335,000	13,500
23	apparel	242,000	30,000
24	lumber and wood	180,000	14,800
25	furniture and fixtures	125,000	−1,400
26	paper	733,000	13,600
27	printing and publishing	64,000	−0,500
28	chemicals	1,722,000	116,700
30	rubber and plastics	779,000	62,600
283	drugs	68,000	3,400
284	cleaning and toilet preparations	28,000	3,200
291	petroleum refining	319,000	15,700
31	leather	68,000	1,100
322	glass	45,000	0,500
32	stone and clay	139,000	5,400
332	iron and steel	341,000	7,500
333	nonferrous metals	525,000	18,400
34	fabricated metal	703,000	57,000
35	machinery and equipment	2306,000	189,400
362	computing equipment	557,000	42,100
36	electrical equipment	2157,000	165,200
363	household appliances	516,000	46,000
367	electric components	1,283,000	119,300
371	motor vehicles and bodies	29,000	7,100
372	motor vehicle parts	1,680,000	103,100
37	transportation equipm.	321,000	32,300
39	miscellaneous manufactures	988,000	89,000
	Total	17,140,000	1,220,000
	Average PACE in percent of output	0.51	0.45

1988 US imports from Mexico in $1000	Expected change of US imports in $1000
81,000	213,300
559,000	92,500
133,000	62,000
506,000	399,800
208,000	20,800
461,000	51,800
342,000	42,700
24,000	1,900
613,000	71,300
324,000	48,300
27,000	2,100
31,000	2,200
204,000	18,700
184,000	30,800
200,000	29,100
286,000	35,200
283,000	48,000
834,000	123,300
469,000	58,600
919,000	113,100
550,000	60,500
2,296,000	370,100
1,368,000	228,000
1,801,000	312,500
1,870,000	191,100
1,331,000	204,000
71,000	6,400
864,000	117,400
16,839,000	2955,500
0.46	0.43

Table 4A.4 Continued

Code	SIC listing	PACE in percent of output	PACE in $1000 of exports
206	sugar	0.360	0,061
20	food	0.330	2,871
22	textiles	0.270	0,905
23	apparel	0.270	0,653
24	lumber and wood	0.330	0,594
25	furniture and fixtures	0.300	0,375
26	paper	1.100	8,063
27	printing and publishing	0.140	0,090
28	chemicals	1.180	20,320
30	rubber and plastics	0.300	2,337
283	drugs	0.500	0,340
284	cleaning and toilet preparations	0.260	0,073
291	petroleum refining	1.620	5,168
31	leather	0.240	0,163
322	glass	0.620	0,279
32	stone and clay	0.700	0,973
332	iron and steel	1.210	4,126
333	nonferrous metals	1.210	6,352
34	fabricated metal	0.480	3,374
35	machinery and equipment	0.180	4,151
362	computing equipment	0.300	1,671
36	electrical equipment	0.450	9,706
363	household appliances	0.290	1,496
367	electric components	0.450	5,773
371	motor vehicles and bodies	0.250	0,072
372	motor vehicle parts	0.250	4,200
37	transportation equipm.	0.280	0,899
39	miscellaneous manufactures	0.220	2,174
	Total		87,260

Expected change of PACE in $1000 of exports	PACE in $1000 of imports	Expected change of PACE in $1000 of imports
−0,003	0,292	0,768
0,217	1,845	0,305
0,036	0,359	0,167
0,081	1,366	1,079
0,049	0,686	0,069
−0,004	1,383	0,155
0,150	3,762	0,470
−0,001	0,034	0,003
1,377	7,233	0,841
0,188	0,972	0,145
0,017	0,135	0,010
0,008	0,081	0,006
0,254	3,305	0,303
0,003	0,442	0,074
0,003	1,240	0,180
0,038	2,002	0,246
0,091	3,424	0,581
0,223	10,091	1,492
0,274	2,251	0,281
0,341	1,654	0,204
0,126	1,650	0,182
0,743	10,332	1,665
0,133	3,967	0,661
0,537	8,104	1,406
0,018	4,675	0,478
0,258	3,328	0,510
0,090	0,199	0,018
0,196	1,901	0,258
5,443	76,713	12,558

5   Economic Integration and the Environment: An Imperfect Competition Approach with Applications to the European Union[1]

5.1 INTRODUCTION

We follow Chapter 4 by investigating the relationship between economic integration and the environment within a model of endogenous policy formation. However, the assumption of perfect competition is given up; we consider large countries which affect each other, and especially their imperfectly competing producers, by the use of environmental policy. More specifically, strategic interaction is explored in two ways: First, by international duopolists, who lobby their governments to influence environmental policy making, and second, by policy makers, who, by environmental regulation, can influence the position of their respective domestic duopolist relative to the position of its foreign competitor.

This chapter is based on previous work on the strategic use of environmental policy, which investigates the use of environmental standards for the enhancement of the competitive standing of domestic producers against foreign rivals. When considering a model of strategically interacting governments and producers, Barrett (1994) finds that policy makers may have incentives to relax environmental standards to suboptimal levels to improve domestic producers' competitive standing. He finds that the danger of a decline of environmental standards for trade reasons mirrors concerns voiced by environmental pressure groups who fear a deterioration of the environment due to free trade. In contrast to Barrett, in this chapter a political-economy approach is introduced and the endogenity of environmental policy with respect to trade policy is explored.

The particular intention of this chapter is to explain how environmental policy is affected by European integration. That is, if the member countries

---

1   This chapter is based on Bommer (1996c).

of the European Union further integrate their markets by removing the last remaining trade obstacles, what can one predict regarding changes in environmental policy? The Common Market affects the condition of the environment in two ways as illustrated by Figure 5.1. First, the Common Market affects the environment directly through changing production and consumption patterns, the first column of Figure 5.1 Such economic effects were investigated in a study of the European Commission, *1992: The Environmental Dimension*, which warns about environmental deterioration (see Task Force, 1990, p. 277). The report of the Task Force predicts that by the year 2010 the completed Common Market will raise emissions of SO_2 by 8–9 percent and emissions of NO_x by 12–14 percent. Further, it expects truck traffic to rise by 30–50 percent, which would increase pollution. According to the Task Force report, rising trade volumes in household waste, hazardous waste and nuclear waste will pose additional problems.

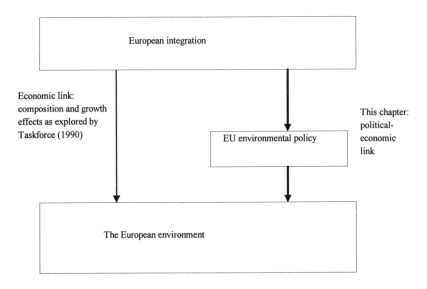

Figure 5.1: The impact of European integration on the environment

The Task Force report examined the environmental effects of economic changes induced by the Common Market project, assuming environmental policy as given. However, EU environmental policy has changed dramatically since its beginnings 25 years ago: EC environmental regulation began in 1967 when the first environmental directive was enacted.[2] A few years later, in 1972, the environmental directorate (DG XI) of the EC was founded (see Vogel, 1995). The amount of EC environmental legislation (regulations, directives and recommendations) has increased drastically over the years. From 1970 to the mid-eighties little more than a 100 items of legislation were passed; by 1992, there was already a total of 450 items enacted. Currently, legislation increases by one hundred items per year (see Vogel, 1995, p. 102 and Pollock Shea, 1993, p. 30).

The growth of environmental regulation in the European Union suggests the necessity of a different approach; environmental policy needs to be endogenized with respect to the Common Market project. This is the political-economic link to the environment which is illustrated by the second column in Figure 5.1. This chapter shows, by applying the endogenous approach to the environment, that EU integration can be associated with improved environmental quality since governments rely on policy instruments to make compensating adjustments to different interest groups, of whom environmentalists are one. The Common Market's driving force for improved environmental standards is the improved ability of policy makers to cooperate through the creation of a single European environmental standard. This contradicts environmentalist fears that Europe's Common-Market project is liable to degrade the environment.

5.2 THE INSTITUTIONAL SET-UP IN THE EUROPEAN UNION

This chapter follows the political-economy approach to European policy making as surveyed by Vaubel (1994). This literature assumes that EU politicians and EU bureaucrats behave according to their own selfish interests, just as consumers and producers are assumed to act in standard neoclassical economic theory. Whereas standard economic analysis is puzzled by the fact that many EU activities, for example, agricultural and structural policies, are redistributive in nature rather than allowing for efficiency improvements, political economy explains why this is the case: political agents choose policies to redistribute rents to interest groups, which, in return, provide services to the agents.[3] Environmental regulation raises the

2   The directive is the most important instrument of EU legislation; it is binding but leaves the member states the choice of form and methods in translating EU laws into national legislation.
3   Peirce (1991) finds that 63 percent of all 1987 expenditures are used for agriculture and 18 percent are used for structural policies. The dominance of distributive measures in the EU can be explained by the importance of political pressure groups in Brussels. Estimates set

same distributional desires and is able to create rents for domestic producers, for example, by lenient environmental regulation, which may improve their competitiveness against foreign rivals.[4]

This chapter focuses on the two institutions, the Commission and the Council, which are most relevant for EU environmental policy making. The influence of the European Parliament, an institution with rather limited political power, is not investigated here.[5] First, the Commission is the agenda setter for issues to be determined in the Council of Ministers. The Commission is modeled as a standard Niskanen-type bureaucracy.[6] It is assumed that the officials of the Commission behave according to their own selfish interests by maximizing their budgets or their influence to improve their personal well-being. To achieve these goals, it is assumed that the officials seek to replace the national regulations of the member states with a single European regulatory body which leads to a uniform standard across the EU. However, the officials of the Commission are limited in their powers because their harmonization proposals have to gain the necessary quorum in the Council.

Second, the Council of Ministers considers the environmental policy proposals of the European Commission. The Council is the most important institution in the EU as all proposed laws pass through this institution, and their adoption is decided mostly by qualified-majority voting or unanimity voting. With regard to environmental policy, the national ministers of the environment have this crucial function. In this chapter, the national policy makers, who meet in the Council, are assumed to maximize their domestic political support or re-election probabilities by deciding whether to introduce national environmental standards or to agree to a single European environmental standard. The model, laid out in the following sections,

the number of interest groups at 3000, of which the majority are of a commercial nature and only a few back social, labor and environmental interests (see Faure and Lefevere, 1994). For some aspects on interest group influence on trade and the environment in the European Union, see Klepper (1992).

4   A separate issue is that of *product standards*, which raises concerns of 'ecoprotectionism'. When the externalities occur from consumption, standards for the protection of the environment usually cover domestic as well as imported products. Lobbying for domestic product standards that exceed those prevailing in the EU may therefore be attractive for domestic producers to reduce competition of competing EU producers. EU rules require harmonized regulations in many cases, but provisions in Articles 100a and 130 allow for leeway concerning environmental solo runs. Since it is hard to discover whether an environmental measure is motivated by environmental or by protectionist intentions, EU environmental regulation provides one of the few loopholes for intra-EU protectionism.

5   The European parliament was not influential under the Single European Act and still has very limited influence under the now prevailing Maastricht treaty rules. The Council of Ministers has the greatest ability to shape Community regulation, a fact confirmed by the analysis of EU decision making with power indexes (see Bindseil and Hantke, 1997).

6   See Vaubel (1994), for the political economy of the European Commission.

incorporates Council and Commission to explore the effects of the Common Market on environmental regulation.

5.3 MODELING THE IMPACT OF EUROPEAN INTEGRATION ON POLLUTION REGULATION

A simple three-stage game investigates the influence of economic integration on European environmental policy in specific sectors of production.[7] This chapter raises the following questions: How is the environment affected by European integration? Is downward competition of standards in the European Union possible? Can European integration induce an EU-wide harmonization of standards on a high level?

To simplify the analysis, Chapter 5 restricts itself to the modeling of two countries, where one depicts the group of EU countries with tight environmental regulations, for example, Germany and Denmark, while the other country represents the group of EU countries with more lenient regulations, for example, the Mediterranean countries and the UK.[8] The three-stage game is structured as follows. In a first stage, which is rather rudimentary, the European Commission develops a proposal for harmonized European environmental regulation. In a second stage, the policy makers of both countries establish pollution standards, maximizing their support from the politically viable interest groups, environmentalists and producers. Finally, in a third stage, domestic and foreign producers choose their levels of output. The model is solved by backward induction.

5.3.1 The Economic Sector

This subsection will analyze the impact of an environmental standard on output and profits in a simple Cournot–Nash game between a domestic and a foreign producer, who are assumed to be the sole producers in the relevant production sector in their respective countries.[9] Both producers are assumed to compete only on the domestic market. This may seem to be a heavy

---

7   There will be no attempt to explain European integration itself because this is done elsewhere. See Schuknecht (1992) for reasons for the development of the Common Market project.

8   Since this is a simplification, the impact of different European decision rules on environmental policy cannot be analyzed. In the two-country setting chosen here, qualified majority rule and unanimity voting end up being the same. Moreover, effects of EU integration and environmental policies on non-members of the European Union are not considered. For this issue, see Rauscher (1992).

9   The market structure is exogenous; there are only two producers who act as duopolists in the one market observed. International aspects come into play when tariffs are introduced.

assumption, but there are two arguments in favor of this approach. First, in reality, we do not observe balanced opportunities of market access for all producers when trade is liberalized. For various reasons, some producers face new opportunities and some face problems regarding market access when liberalization takes place. Thus, this is the simplest way of modeling losers and winners of trade liberalization that are crucial for this political-economy study. Second, other studies on trade and the environment rely on similarly restrictive settings. Ludema and Wooton (1994), who analyzed trade and environment issues in competitive markets, apply the same production-consumption structure: a single foreign and a domestic producer compete only on the domestic market. Other literature in the trade and environment field has applied rather restrictive settings. Barrett (1994), for instance, examines the competition of producers from two countries on a third market without considering consumption in the two countries at all.

Each producer maximizes his or her profits according to

$$\max_{x^i} \Pi^i = (q^i - c^i - k^i) x^i \text{, with } i = d, f .$$ (5.1)

Π^i stands for the profits of the respective producer, q^i represents the market price, c^i are the unit production cost, k^i gives the unit cost of compliance with the pollution standard and x^i denotes output. The domestic inverse demand curve

$$q^d = \frac{A - \Sigma x^i}{2}$$ (5.2)

is negatively sloped, with A portraying market size. Both producers sell only on the domestic market, which is protected by a tariff t. For this homogeneous duopoly, the law of one price implies:

$$q^f = q^d - t .$$ (5.3)

According to equation (5.3), q^d, the price of the home producer, is higher than q^f, the price of the foreign producer. Equation (5.4) defines k^i, the unit cost of complying with the pollution standard v^i, where the pollution standard is defined as limit of pollution per unit of production.[10] The polluting industry will always utilize the environment to the maximum amount

10 I refrain from analyzing fix-cost components of pollution control. Cost of pollution control for the firm are strictly variable, for example, contaminated or hazardous waste of production which is given away for treatment and disposal. With increasing degree of treatment undertaken, costs rise exponentially.

possible; therefore, in the subsequent analysis the pollution standard is always equivalent to the pollution actually emitted. The superscript of v^i indicates that the standards are set independently in the two countries. The pollution standard is binding, because the exploitation of all legal pollution opportunities minimizes unit abatement cost.

$$k^i = \frac{1}{v^i}, \text{ with } i = d, f \,.$$

(5.4)

k^i increases with the tightness of the standard at an increasing rate: $k^i_{v^i} < 0, k^i_{v^i v^i} > 0$.

The solution of the game exhibits standard results of Cournot–Nash competition. The reaction functions of both producers are negatively sloped and linear. Equilibrium output and profit for both producers increase with the severity of the other country's environmental standard whereas output and profit decrease with the tightness of the own standard. The domestic tariff drives up the domestic producer's output and profits, but reduces output and profits of the foreign rival. I obtain the following equilibrium output and profit levels of the domestic producer for a given pollution standard:

$$x^d = \frac{1}{3}(A - 4c^d - 4/v^d + 2t + 2c^f + 2/v^f)$$

(5.5)

and

$$\Pi^d = \frac{1}{2}(x^d)^2.$$

(5.6)

The output and profit levels of the foreign producer are as follows:

$$x^f = \frac{1}{3}(A - 4c^f - 4/v^f - 4t + 2c^d + 2/v^d)$$

(5.7)

and

$$\Pi^f = \frac{1}{2}(x^f)^2.$$

(5.8)

5.3.2 The Political Sector

The regulating bodies which set the pollution standard in each country, consist of politicians who seek to maximize political support via their environmental policy. Support is due to the two major interests, the producers and the environmentalists. Following Stigler's (1971) and

Peltzman's (1976) theory of regulation, I argue that the policy maker of country i maximizes the following political support function with respect to v^i:

$$\max_{v^i} M^i = f\left[\Pi^i\left(v^i\right), V^i(v^i)\right], \text{ with } i = d, f.$$ (5.9)

V^i represents absolute pollution in country i:

$$V^i = v^i x^i,$$ (5.10)

which determines the political support from the environmental pressure groups. The politician faces a trade-off when setting the pollution standard: a tight standard delivers support from environmentalists but raises opposition from the producer. The support function is supposed to have the standard concavity properties: marginal political support of the producer from a lenient pollution standard v^i is positive, but diminishing when the pollution limit is expanded $(M_v > 0,\ M_{vv} < 0)$. The marginal political support from the environmentalists is decreasing with a lenient standard v^i. Pollution is purely local, it does not affect foreign production or the utility of foreign environmentalists, but provides disutility only for the domestic environmental interests.[11]

I employ the following explicit political support function

$$M^i = \sqrt{\Pi^i} - \alpha^i V^i,$$ (5.11)

with the concavity properties mentioned above. Political support of the environmentalists depends on absolute domestic pollution V^i and on their weight in the political process α^i. α^i is large in the country group mentioned, having strong and politically influential environmental interest groups, such as the Netherlands, Denmark and Germany, as opposed to the Mediterranean countries and the UK, where a low α indicates a weaker influence of environmentalists. The trade-off for the politician is depicted in Figure 5.2; a tight pollution standard increases support from environmentalists as V^i falls, but reduces support from producers as profits fall.

---

11   Here, environmentalists are greens, meaning they are only concerned with domestic environmental quality, as opposed to supergreens, who also care for the environment elsewhere. For the distinction between greens and supergreens and their influence on trade policy, see Hillman and Ursprung (1992, 1994).

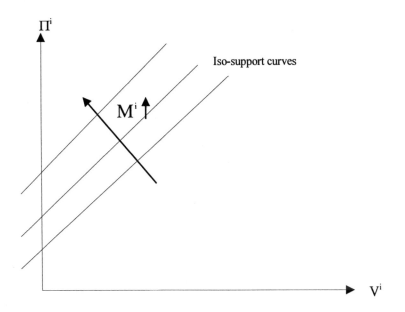

Figure 5.2: *The politicians' trade-off*

Substituting equation (5.10) and the equilibrium profit functions of the second stage of the game, (5.6) and (5.8), into equation (5.11), one obtains

$$\max_{v^i} M^i = \sqrt{\frac{1}{2}} \cdot x^i(v^i) - \alpha^i v^i x^i(v^i). \tag{5.12}$$

Maximizing M^i with respect to v^i and subject to the constraints (5.5) and (5.7), respectively, yields the following reaction function for the home country

$$v^d(v^f) = \frac{(8)^{1/4}}{[\alpha^d(A - 4c^d + 2t + 2c^f + 2/v^f)]^{1/2}} . \tag{5.13}$$

For the foreign country, one obtains a symmetric reaction function

$$v^f(v^d) = \frac{(8)^{1/4}}{[\alpha^f(A - 4c^f - 4t + 2c^d + 2/v^d)]^{1/2}} . \tag{5.14}$$

The two restrictions $x^i \geq 0$ and $M^i \geq 0$ are necessary to guarantee an interior solution. The first restriction, $x^i \geq 0$, obtained by setting (5.5) and (5.7) to zero and solving them with respect to v^i, is depicted by equations (5.15) and (5.16). This restriction excludes solutions which generate negative output and are characterized through exploding costs due to a very tight environmental regulation.

$$\hat{v}^d = \frac{4}{A - 4c^d + 2t + 2c^f + 2/v^f} \tag{5.15}$$

and

$$\hat{v}^f = \frac{4}{A - 4c^f - 4t + 2c^d + 2/v^d}. \tag{5.16}$$

Figure 5.3 illustrates that a standard $\hat{v}^d$ should not be exceeded to satisfy restrictions (5.15) and (5.16), otherwise output and political support become negative. As well, the restrictions (5.15) and (5.16) are depicted in Figure 5.3 by dotted lines and exclude solutions which are located in the south-western part of Figure 5.4.

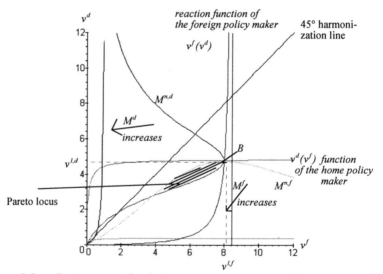

Figure 5.3:   *Environmental policies prior to integration if the environmentalists are more powerful in the home country*

The second restriction, $M^i \geq 0$, requires that political support is non-negative. Substituting equations (5.5) and (5.7) into equation (5.12) and setting equation (5.12) to zero and solving it with respect to v^i gives the values for v^i which guarantee that $M^i \geq 0$:

$$\widetilde{v}^i = \frac{1}{\alpha^i \cdot \sqrt{2}}. \tag{5.17}$$

Figure 5.4 illustrates that the environmental standard should not fall short of $\widetilde{v}^i$, otherwise political support becomes negative.

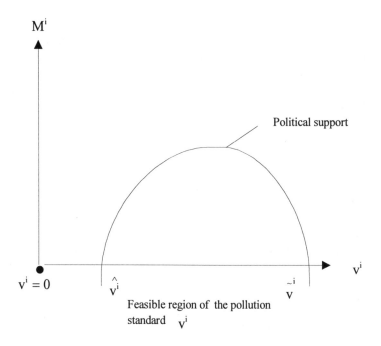

Figure 5.4:   Feasible region of the pollution standard

If the above restrictions are not satisfied, the policy makers choose the corner solution: a standard of $v^i = 0$, which prohibits production and provides the political support $M^i = 0$.[12]

---

12 A case where environmental regulation induced a discontinuation of production, is nuclear power in Germany. The construction of new nuclear power plants came to a halt for environmental reasons.

5.4   THE EUROPEAN ENVIRONMENTAL POLICY EQUILIBRIUM

Environmental policies are chosen in the two countries by policy makers, who maximize their respective political support by balancing the requirements of domestic interest groups. Producers demand a lenient environmental standard not only for cost and profit reasons, but also because their competitiveness against the foreign producer is strengthened. Two points have to be made prior to the explanation of European environmental policy, which is illustrated in Figure 5.3.

First, countries differ in the strength of their environmentalist pressure groups and in the trading position of their producers, as explained below. Second, this chapter follows the institutional framework as described in Section 5.2: politicians meet in the Council of Ministers and decide whether to set standards independently or whether to have a common European environmental policy. The EU Commission has the power of initiating this common policy and it is assumed that the Commission has a strong preference for the harmonization of standards for bureaucratic reasons. From this it follows that the Commission initiates a proposal only if the proposal calls for a single EU-wide standard.

Two cases have to be considered: (i) the import-competing home country has a stronger environmental movement than the exporting foreign country; and (ii) the environmental movement is stronger in the foreign country. For the former case, Figure 5.3 depicts a numerical simulation of the environmental-policy equilibrium, before integration of the economies takes place. The following parameter values are used: $\alpha^d = 0.012$, $\alpha^f = 0.01$, $c^i = 1, A = 10, t = 1$.

Point B depicts the equilibrium of European environmental policy, the point where the home and foreign reaction functions cross. In equilibrium, both countries have different environmental standards, depicted through the non-cooperative equilibrium in Figure 5.3, where the home standard $v^{1,d}$ is stricter than the foreign standard $v^{1,f}$. The non-cooperative-equilibrium standards depend positively on the profits of the producers and on the political power of the environmentalists. Differentiating the reaction function of the home government (5.13) with respect to the tariff t and to the environmentalists' influence α, the reaction function shifts downward for both variables. A stronger environmental pressure group raises the pollution standard, given the foreign standard. In the same fashion, trade protection provides shelter for the home producer from foreign competition, boosts his or her profits, and enables the government to tighten the home standard. Since the home producer is better off through trade protection, the government can impose the burden of tighter pollution regulation on the producer. On the other hand, domestic trade protection weakens the foreign producer by lowering his or her output and profits. The foreign reaction function (5.14) shifts upward. The foreign government compensates the foreign producer by a less costly, more lenient environmental standard.[13]

The existence of the Pareto locus illustrates the downward competition of standards in the non-cooperative equilibrium in point B. Politicians face a prisoner's dilemma; each politician seeks to relax the home standard to improve the home producers position against his or her foreign rival. If politicians could establish their environmental standards cooperatively, domestic and foreign politicians would choose the cooperative standards, which are tighter than the non-cooperative standards $v^{1,d}$ and $v^{1,f}$. Both politicians would prefer to cooperate because cooperation induces a higher political support compared to political support in the non-cooperative solution. Cooperation enables politicians to reach higher iso-political support curves, which deliver more political support than the iso-political support curves $M^{n,d}$ and $M^{n,f}$ from the non-cooperative solution.

Since national environmental standards differ considerably in the non-cooperative equilibrium depicted in point B, neither cooperation nor harmonization is possible. Cooperation is not possible because each policy maker has an incentive to deviate from the cooperative equilibrium. An alternative to cooperation, harmonization of policies by a shift of environmental policy making to a supra-national institution, could solve the politicians' prisoner's dilemma. Harmonization requires that both policy makers accept a harmonization proposal ($v^d = v^f$) of the Commission, a requirement which is not agreed upon because it is not Pareto-superior. At least one policy maker would be worse off if accepting the harmonization proposal, and would turn it down. This is illustrated in Figure 5.3, indicating that harmonized policy solutions (the harmonization line) are not within the Pareto locus. Therefore, the only possible solution is depicted by point B. The policy makers have to stick to their own national non-cooperative

---

13 In the set-up of this book, domestic political decisions affect not only domestic interest groups, but foreign groups as well. For instance, the tightening up of domestic environmental control raises the profits of the foreign producer and, consequently, the level of foreign political support. An alternative way of modeling the channels which influence the level of political support of governments is presented by Hillman (1982). In his set-up, domestic support depends only on the policies selected by the domestic government. More specifically, political support depends only on the gains and losses which are due to the authorities' policy changes; support does not depend on the absolute utility levels of interest groups.

equilibrium environmental standards, which are lower than their politically optimal standards.[14]

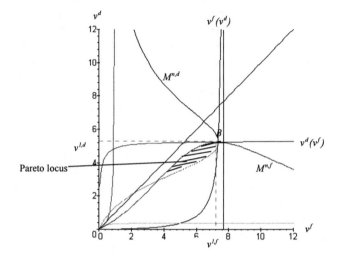

Figure 5.5:   *Environmental policies prior to integration if the environmentalists are more powerful in the foreign country*

Up until now, it was assumed that the home country has more influential environmentalists than the foreign country. In contrast, if the foreign country has the more influential environmental movement ($\alpha^d < \alpha^f$), the equilibrium is less clear-cut than shown in Figure 5.3. Two opposing effects, which shape environmental regulation, are at work. In the home country, weak environmentalists affect the pollution standard negatively, shifting the foreign reaction function (5.14) upward. But trade protection provides shelter for the home producer from foreign competition, boosts his or her profits, and enables the government to tighten the home standard. Effects are the opposite in the foreign country. Domestic trade protection weakens the foreign producer by lowering his or her output and profits. Falling profits exert pressure to relax the foreign standard. On the other hand, there is pressure to raise the foreign standard because the foreign environmental pressure groups exert more influence than their domestic counterparts on

---

14 However, the inability to solve the cooperation problem depends on the necessity to cooperate by means of a single European standard. If this assumption is relaxed by allowing for minimum standards in European policy making, cooperation could be achieved even if non-cooperative standards are very divergent.

their respective governments. Figure 5.5 gives a numerical example for the parameter values $\alpha^d = 0.01, \alpha^f = 0.012, c^i = 1, A = 10, t = 1$.

Figure 5.5 shows that, in equilibrium, which is marked by the point B, the foreign standard is more lenient than the home standard. Trade protection exerts a heavier downward pressure on the foreign environmental standard than the environmentalists in the foreign country, who are stronger than in the home country, and exert upward pressure on the foreign standard – at least under the parameter values used here.

5.5 EUROPEAN INTEGRATION

If the environmentalists are stronger in the home (import-competing) country, integration improves the access of the foreign producer to the home market. The various aspects of integration inside the EU, the abolition of tariffs, non-tariff barriers and restrictions on public procurement for foreign firms, are modeled for reasons of simplicity by reducing the tariff t, which splits the foreign and the home producer's price prior to integration. According to equation (5.18) the domestic reaction function shifts upward. Since access to the home market is easier, integration weakens the domestic producer, who is compensated by more lenient domestic environmental regulation, given the foreign regulatory standard:

$$\frac{\partial v^d}{\partial t} = -\frac{(8)^{1/4}}{(\alpha^d)^{1/2}(A - 4c^d + 2t + 2c^f + 2/v^f)^{3/2}} < 0. \tag{5.18}$$

On the other hand, the competitive standing of the foreign producer is enhanced. According to equation (5.19) the foreign reaction function shifts downward. The foreign government sets tighter environmental regulation, given the home standard.

$$\frac{\partial v^f}{\partial t} = \frac{2 \cdot (8)^{1/4}}{(\alpha^f)^{1/2}(A - 4c^f - 4t + 2c^d + 2/v^d)^{3/2}} > 0. \tag{5.19}$$

The shift of the two reaction functions is illustrated in Figure 5.6. Integration leads to the new equilibrium point C, where the home standard is more lenient ($\partial v^f / \partial t > 0$) and the foreign standard is more tight ($\partial v^d / \partial t < 0$). This is shown in Appendix 5A.1.

The explicit modeling of the political processes in both countries shows that environmental regulation is endogenous to economic integration. Inasmuch as the policy makers balance the politically viable interests of both integrating countries, pollution standards converge to a certain extent, but still keep the standard tighter in the home country, the country with the more influential environmental pressure group ($v^{2,d} < v^{2,f}$). The result of economic integration is depicted in Figure 5.6 by a shift of the environmental-policy equilibrium from point B (the equilibrium point in Figure 5.3) to the new non-cooperative equilibrium point C. The following parameter values are retained, only the tariff rate t is set to zero: $\alpha^d = 0.012, \alpha^f = 0.01,\ c^i = 1, A = 10, t = 0$.

In the non-cooperative solution, both policy makers are caught in a political prisoner's dilemma. Downward competition of their environmental standards improves the competitive standing of their producers, a result which mirrors the predictions of the literature on the strategic use of environmental policy cited in Section 5.1.

However, European integration implies other effects than the shift to the new non-cooperative equilibrium in point C. As mentioned in Section 5.1, integration has led to a major shift to harmonized EU legislation on the environment, explained by the Commission's preference for harmonized policy solutions. But only the convergence of the economies enables the convergence of standards. Integration shifts the Pareto-superior allocations of both policy makers in the area of harmonized standards (Figure 5.6). Now, the Commission is able to use its agenda-setting power to successfully propose harmonized legislation. Both policy makers agree to the Commission's proposal since the proposal is part of the Pareto-superior allocations. The new harmonized standard is illustrated in Figure 5.6 by the part of the 45° harmonization line between point D and F, which is part of the Pareto-superior allocations. In contrast to the non-cooperative solution, a harmonized solution helps to overcome the political prisoner's dilemma and results in a tighter single standard than the non-cooperative-solution standards in the two countries (point C).[15] The foreign standard will be tightened with integration. However, the question whether the harmonized standard will be tighter in the home country as well, remains unresolved. The home standard will be tighter only if the Commission initiates a proposal between point E and point F.

---

15 Appendix 5A2 presents simulation results where harmonization is not possible.

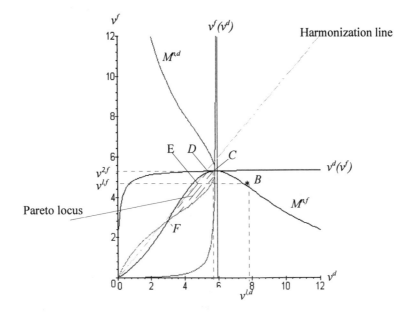

Figure 5.6: *Policy harmonization after integration if the environmentalists are more powerful in the home country*

As in the preceding scenario, the foreign producer gains, which allows the foreign government to set higher standards. The home producer suffers from increasing competition from the foreign producer, induced by economic integration, and is therefore compensated by weaker standards. Environmental regulations converge increasingly, making a single European environmental policy possible as well. The following parameter values are retained from Figure 5.5, only the tariff rate t is set to zero: $\alpha^D = 0.01, \alpha^F = 0.012, \ c^i = 1, \ A = 10, \ t = 0$.

Converging environmental regulations are illustrated in Figure 5.7 by the upward shift of the home reaction function and a downward shift of the foreign reaction function. This is depicted by the shift from the old equilibrium B to the new equilibrium C, where the foreign standard is stricter than the home standard.

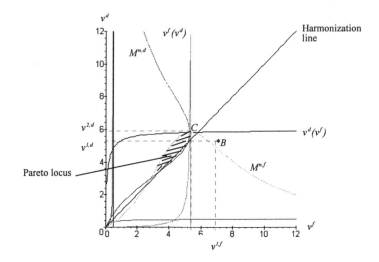

*Figure 5.7:   Policy harmonization after integration if the environmentalists
are more powerful in the foreign country*

In contrast to the convergence result obtained above, trade integration may
induce the divergence of standards. This is the case if the influence of
environmentalists relative to the producers is large. Then, prior to integration,
standards in both countries could be similar. Integration induces the
divergence of regulations as the foreign standard goes up, whereas the home
standard declines.

5.6 DOES THE COMMON MARKET INCREASE POLLUTION?

Up until now we have considered the effect of integration on pollution
standards in both countries. But what can we predict regarding environmental
quality in general? The pollution standard gives only an upper limit to
pollution per unit of production. For effects of integration on absolute
pollution, changes in the output in each country have to be observed, as
indicated by equation (5.10).

According to equation (5.18), trade liberalization shifts the reaction
function of the home pollution standard upward, indicating a more lenient
environmental standard.[16] At the same time, production falls:

---

16   This section considers the case of a country with an import-competing producer and a
strong environmental movement.

$$\frac{\partial x^d}{\partial t} = \frac{2}{3} > 0.$$

(5.20)

The effect on the home country's environment is ambiguous since a lower standard worsens environmental conditions, whereas falling output eases the pressure on the environment. Comparing (5.18) and (5.20), it can be seen that environmental conditions improve if α^d is large. A strong domestic environmental movement helps to improve the domestic environment, which compensates the negative effect of trade liberalization on $v^d(v^f)$. While output effects are independent from α^d, a high α^d reduces the political influence of producers, making their demand for compensation with a lenient standard less successful: environmental regulation falls only a little.

The effect on the foreign country's environment is ambiguous as well: according to equation (5.19), the foreign policy maker tightens the standard if trade is liberalized. On the other hand, output increases (equation (5.21)). The environment benefits from tight regulation, but suffers from higher output:

$$\frac{\partial x^f}{\partial t} = -\frac{4}{3} < 0.$$

(5.21)

Comparing (5.19) and (5.21), it can be seen that environmental conditions improve if α^f is small; a weak foreign environmental movement helps to improve the foreign environment. While output effects are independent from α^f, a low α^f increases the political power of the producer and, consequently, induces a low environmental standard in the pre-integration equilibrium. But as this producer profits from trade liberalization, the share of his or her gains, which is transformed into tighter regulation, is positively related to his or her weight in the political process: the higher the weight, the more he or she has to give away for redistribution. Therefore, a small α^f improves the environment.

However, if we observe a less powerful environmentalist lobby in the home country, the home standard declines even further from the low pre-integration level and may induce a deterioration of the domestic environment. In this set-up, the foreign environment is adversely affected for a different reason. If the foreign environmental lobby is stronger than assumed above, then the improvement of the foreign standard is not sufficient to compensate for the adverse environmental effect of increasing output. However, the possible deterioration of the environment relies on the downward competition of standards as described in Section 5.4. If standards converge in the process of integration, politicians are able to cooperate and increase their political support by tightening standards. Then, the effect on the environment may be beneficial: by tightening standards, production declines and reduces pollution in general (see equation (5.10)).[17]

5.7 INTERNATIONAL POLLUTION SPILLOVERS

To a large extent, EU environmental problems are not limited to the countries in which pollution originates. The cross-border nature of pollution in the Rhine and SO_2 emissions, for instance, shows the EU-wide dimension of environmental problems.[18] Therefore, part of the environmental regulation in the EU, for example, the Large Combustion Directive, aims at solving cross-border pollution problems affecting several member states.[19] The investigation of cross-border pollution issues is straightforward.

Political support depends on the profits of the domestic producer and on absolute pollution of domestic and of foreign origin affecting each country. It is assumed that environmentalists are concerned only with domestic environmental quality, ignoring the environmental effects of domestic pollution on the foreign country. Political support is maximized according to

$$M^d = \sqrt{\Pi}^d - \alpha^d \cdot [\beta^d \cdot v^d \cdot x^d + (1-\beta^f) \cdot v^f \cdot x^f] \qquad (5.22)$$

for the home country, and for the foreign country by

$$M^f = \sqrt{\Pi}^f - \alpha^f \cdot [\beta^f \cdot v^f \cdot x^f + (1-\beta^d) \cdot v^d \cdot x^d]. \qquad (5.23)$$

Since pollution is transboundary, only a share of domestic emissions, indicated by β^d, causes harm domestically and the share of foreign emissions β^f causes harm in the foreign country. The remaining emissions $(1-\beta^d)$ and $(1-\beta^f)$ are of a cross-border nature and cause harm in the foreign country and in the home country, respectively.

---

17 However, the issue is more complicated. There is a side-effect of integration with regard to output changes: even though stricter standards reduce output, free trade increases the collective output of the two countries.

18 See Kirchgässner (1992) for an overview of transboundary environmental problems in the EU and for solution concepts.

19 The 1988 Large Combustion Directive requires shrubbers in coal-fired plants to reduce dust, SO_2 and NO_X emissions.

The reaction functions of the two governments are analogous to the reactions functions (5.13) and (5.14) in the case of purely domestic pollution. The reaction function of the home country is

$$v^d(v^f) = \frac{[(8)^{1/2} + 2 \cdot \alpha^d (1 - \beta^f) v^f]^{1/2}}{[\alpha^d \cdot \beta^d (A - 4c^d + 2t + 2c^f + 2/v^f)]^{1/2}}. \qquad (5.24)$$

For the foreign country the symmetric reaction function is

$$v^f(v^d) = \frac{[(8)^{1/2} + 2 \cdot \alpha^f (1 - \beta^d) v^d]^{1/2}}{[\alpha^f \cdot \beta^f (A - 4c^f - 4t + 2c^d + 2/v^d)]^{1/2}}. \qquad (5.25)$$

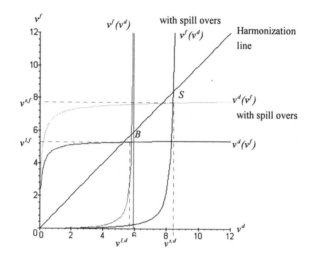

Figure 5.8:   International pollution spillovers

The non-cooperative equilibrium for the two pollution standards is depicted by point S in Figure 5.8. With international pollution spillovers, both standards are more lenient than in the case of purely domestic pollution, illustrated by point B. In the case of purely domestic pollution, politicians face only one prisoner's dilemma. Politicians reduce pollution standards below politically optimal levels to improve the competitiveness of the domestic producer. Politicians face a second prisoner's dilemma when pollution crosses national borders. Each country 'exports' a share of domestic pollution to the other country without having to bear the cost of the damage this causes in the other country. Such an international environmental externality induces excess pollution and reduces pollution standards even further below politically optimal levels, as illustrated by point S. The larger the shares of spill-overs ($1-\beta^d$ and $1-\beta^f$), the higher the externality and the lower is the non-cooperative equilibrium in environmental regulation. Figure 5.8 gives a numerical example for the parameter values $\alpha^d = 0.012, \alpha^f = 0.01, \ c^i = 1, \ A = 10, t = 1$ and $\beta^i = 0.5$.

Regarding EU integration, results are qualitatively the same for international pollution spillovers as depicted in Figures 5.3 and 5.6 for the case of pure domestic pollution. EU integration induces a convergence of pollution standards if the country with the powerful environmental lobby has an import-competing producer. Convergence is the condition which finally enables a tight EU-wide pollution standard.

5.8 CONCLUSION

This chapter shows that the endogenity of environmental policy with respect to trade integration affects results considerably. Like other studies examining the incentives of policy makers to lower environmental standards to suboptimal low levels, this chapter found that downward competition of standards is possible. This is caused by the fact that environmental regulation not only raises the producer's cost, but reduces his or her competitiveness with respect to his or her foreign competitor. However, in this chapter it was shown that European integration is able to overcome this politicians' prisoner's dilemma of lower than politically optimal pollution standards. European integration enables the politicians to cooperate in environmental policy making by the creation of a single European pollution standard. The results obtained are as follows.

The removal of trade barriers induces a *convergence* of pollution standards if the country with the powerful environmental lobby has an import-competing producer. The policy maker of the country with the powerful environmental pressure group relaxes the pollution standard to compensate the domestic producer for losses due to foreign competition. The policy maker of the country with the weak environmental movement sets a tighter standard because the local producer, gaining from economic integration, is now better able to cope with environmental regulation.

Convergence enables the Commission to initiate legislation for a single European standard which is accepted by the policy makers of both countries. The single European standard is tighter than uncoordinated national regulation, because it helps to overcome the political prisoner's dilemma of the national policy makers, who downgrade their standards to raise domestic producers' profits. The drastic increase of EU legislation on the environment in recent years suggests that the convergence result is a likely outcome. But empirical examination would be particularly desirable to determine whether the trade–environment relationships described in fact determine the evolution of EU environmental policy.

Hence, fears that European integration induces a deterioration of the environment are not justified. Integration may put a strain on the environment by increasing economic activity, but forces which strengthen environmental regulation could become more powerful. Furthermore, the European environment may improve since the pro-environmental interests in the Council are strengthened because of admission into the EU of countries with influential environmental pressure groups, such as Austria, Sweden and Finland.

APPENDIX 5A1: PROOF OF THE EFFECTS OF INTEGRATION ON POLLUTION STANDARDS

We determine the effects of trade liberalization on the pollution standard in both countries by solving the system of the two equations (5.13) and (5.14) with respect to the tariff rate t according to Cramer's rule:

$$\frac{\partial v^d}{\partial t} = \frac{1}{|J|} \underbrace{\begin{vmatrix} 2\alpha^d & 2\alpha^d / (v^f)^2 \\ -4\alpha^f & -\sqrt{\tfrac{1}{2}} \cdot 8 / (v^f)^3 \end{vmatrix}}_{|A|} \tag{5A1.1}$$

and

$$\frac{\partial v^f}{\partial t} = \frac{1}{|J|} \underbrace{\begin{vmatrix} -\sqrt{\tfrac{1}{2}} \cdot 8 / (v^d)^3 & 2\alpha^d \\ 2\alpha^f / (v^d)^2 & -4\alpha^f \end{vmatrix}}_{|B|}, \tag{5A1.2}$$

where the Jacobian determinant

$$|J| = \begin{vmatrix} -\sqrt{\tfrac{1}{2}} \cdot 8 / (v^d)^3 & 2\alpha^d & 2\alpha^d / (v^f)^2 \\ 2\alpha^f / (v^d)^2 & -4\alpha^f & -\sqrt{\tfrac{1}{2}} \cdot 8 / (v^f)^3 \end{vmatrix}.$$

The domestic pollution standard becomes more lenient ($\partial v^d / \partial t < 0$) if two conditions are satisfied: (i) $|A|$ has to be negative; (ii) the Jacobian determinant has to be positive.

Solving $|A| < 0$ induces

$$v^f < \frac{\sqrt{2}}{\alpha^f}. \tag{5A1.3}$$

The positive political-support constraint (5.15) requires that $v^f < 1/\alpha^f \sqrt{2}$ which is more restrictive than is (5A1.3). The minimum standard v required by (5.15) is tighter than the required v in (5A1.3). Therefore (i) is satisfied.

Solving $|J| > 0$ induces

$$v^d < \frac{8}{\alpha^d v^f \alpha^f} . \qquad (5A1.4)$$

Substituting (5A1.3) into (5A1.4) induces

$$v^d < \frac{4 \cdot \sqrt{2}}{\alpha^d} , \qquad (5A1.5)$$

which is less restrictive than the positive political-support constraint (5.15).[20] Therefore $|J| > 0$ is satisfied.

Integration tightens the foreign pollution standard ($\partial v^f / \partial t > 0$) if two conditions are satisfied: (i) the Jacobian has to be positive, which has been proved above; (ii) $|B|$ has to be positive. Solving $|B| > 0$ gives

$$v^d < \frac{4 \cdot \sqrt{2}}{\alpha^d} . \qquad (5A1.6)$$

The positive political support constraint (5.15) requires that $v^d < 1/\alpha^d \sqrt{2}$ which is more restrictive than is (5A1.6). The minimum standard v required by (5.15) is tighter than the required v in (5A1.6). Therefore (ii) is satisfied.

---

20 This is the case of $v^f = \sqrt{2} / \alpha^f$. For more restrictive values of v^f, equation (5A1.5) becomes less restrictive and satisfies $|J| > 0$ as well.

APPENDIX 5A2:   THE CASE OF COUNTRIES IN WHICH PRESSURE GROUP INFLUENCE DIFFERS CONSIDERABLY

Appendix 5A.2 considers whether the cooperation result of Section 5.5 can be retained if both countries differ with regard to the political impact of environmentalists to a higher extent than assumed in Section 5.5. The following parameter values $\alpha^d = 0.02$, $\alpha^f = 0.01$, $c^i = 1$, $A = 10$, $t = 1$ are used, whereby the impact of the environmentalists in the home country is double ($\alpha^d = 0.02$) the impact in the foreign country ($\alpha^f = 0.01$). Figure 5A2.1 shows the pre-integration equilibrium, in which the home standard is tighter than the foreign standard.

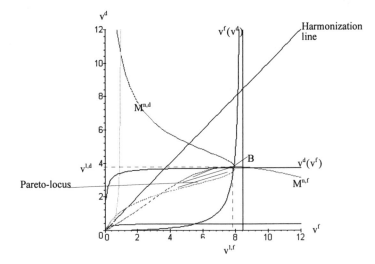

Figure 5A2.1:   Environmental policies prior to integration if the environmentalists are more powerful in the home country

European integration, illustrated by Figure 5A2.2, is simulated by the removal of the tariff *t*, which is reduced from the pre-integration value of one to the value of zero.

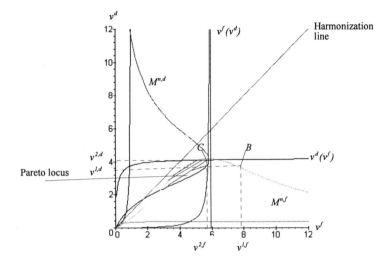

Figure 5A2.2:   *Policy harmonization after integration if the environmentalists are more powerful in the home country*

Figure 5A2.2 shows that standards converge to a certain extent when trade is liberalized, but the convergence is not large enough to shift the Pareto locus on the harmonization line. Hence, the European Commission will fail to make a harmonization proposal which is accepted by both policy makers. The prisoner's dilemma prevails; environmental standards are lower than politically efficient. The environmentalist impact in both countries is too different to induce a convergence which is sufficient to make a cooperation result possible.

6 Economic Integration and the Environment: Imperfect Competition and Asymmetric Information[1]

6.1 INTRODUCTION

Chapter 5 has considered the case of the strategic competition of governments to enhance the competitiveness of domestic producers against their foreign rivals. It was shown that the governments are trapped in a non-cooperative equilibrium in which they set lower than efficient environmental standards. Furthermore, it was shown that this prisoner's dilemma can be overcome through economic and political integration. In that set-up, the government has perfect information regarding the production decisions of the producers: the government knows exactly what a certain pollution standard would do to the producers. Chapter 6 renounces this assumption by assuming that the government has only limited information about the ability of domestic producers to cope with a possible environmental standard. To emphasize the strategic interaction under asymmetric information between producers and government, this chapter will be limited to model only a small open economy where only one producer, a monopolist, is affected by environmental regulation. In contrast to the previous chapters, the focus is on the effects of environmental policies on investment decisions of producers and, more specifically, the question of whether domestic firms relocate their production abroad. Furthermore, this chapter asks how such location decisions are affected by free trade.

The unilateral increase of environmental control has frequently been objected to on the grounds that domestic firms may lose their competitive edge to foreign competitors not subject to these restrictions. According to this line of reasoning, domestic firms shift their production, and hence employment, to countries with less-restrictive environmental standards. This is called the 'pollution-haven hypothesis'. Recent examples include furniture manufacturers who moved from the Los Angeles area to Mexico allegedly

1   This chapter is based on Bommer (1998).

125

because of the stricter air emission laws in the US (see Hufbauer and Schott, 1992, pp. 150). Other producers shut down specific product lines or entire plants. The two chemical companies Hoechst and Bayer, for example, have closed production for certain chemicals in Germany because of strict environmental standards (see Voss, 1993, pp. 31–2).[2]

Should policy makers really be concerned that a stricter environmental policy will bring about a substantial relocation of capital? This chapter focuses on this issue. In particular, it is shown that following an increase in environmental standards, firms may shift part of their production abroad for strategic reasons rather than because of a loss of competitiveness. That is, capital export is used as a means of indirect rent seeking to signal to the government an alleged low competitiveness at home, while its real intention is to avoid costly clean-up investment in the future. Indirect lobbying is one of the means of influencing trade policy. In contrast to direct lobbying, real changes in production, for example, layoffs and plant closings, are used to lobby for protection.[3]

This chapter considers explicitly the asymmetry of information between regulator and regulatee, an aspect which was neglected by the trade and environment literature reviewed in Chapter 2. The administration setting environmental standards does not know to what extent the firms are affected by its regulation, in particular since firms are heterogeneous in their ability to adapt to higher levels of environmental control.[4] Since a political-support-maximizing government balances the interests of the relevant lobbying groups at the margin, regulation will be less stringent, the more severe the companies' losses in terms of output and employment are. Firms can take advantage of that and may, subsequent to an enhancement of environmental standards, relocate production abroad for strategic reasons only: by signaling low adaptability they may convince the government to refrain from a further increase of environmental control. This chapter explores the possibility of indirect rent seeking analytically in a signaling game, and it will be demonstrated under what circumstances the firm will be able to deceive the government about its ability to adapt to higher standards. In particular, it

2 See Chapter 2, Subsection 2.2.3 for more examples of environmental regulation which have a significant impact on relocation decisions of firms, in particular on pollution-intensive sectors of production.

3 One case is *spurious injury*. Since the injury criterion is a necessary condition to obtain protection under contingent protection rules, import-competing firms may use *spurious injury* to qualify for protection. For a survey on indirect protection, see Leidy (1994).

4 A different setting of asymmetric information, where producers have imperfect information regarding the government's choice of environmental policy, is considered by Cadot and Sinclair-Desgagné (1995). In their set-up, the government can commit to regulatory change, but cannot commit to the date of the change. They find that such regulatory uncertainty is an incentive device to induce domestic firms to invest in the development of new technologies.

emerges that trade liberalization causes a more frequent use of strategic relocation. This eases the compensation of the producer for losses caused by trade liberalization, which occur as competition with foreign rivals becomes more intense.

6.2 THE MODEL

6.2.1 The Framework

A simple model is presented to illustrate the central features of the interaction between a government which sets a pollution limit and a producer who chooses technology and output. I keep the model as simple as possible to allow for the complexity which arises by introducing uncertainty and dynamic aspects in the subsequent sections.

The policy maker specifies the limit on purely domestic environmental pollution V, to maximize his or her political support M according to the following function:

$$\max_{V} M = f\left[(X(V),U(V)\right].\tag{6.1}$$

There is a trade-off for the policy maker between high support from output interests X and support from environmentalists U. Strict pollution regulation of the policy maker (a low V) increases support from environmentalists, but reduces support from the consumer interests. These interests can be thought of as consumers who gain from an abundant supply of goods. In a similar fashion, labor interests, which are not modeled explicitly, gain from high output if one assumes a strong correlation between employment and output. The support function has the standard concavity properties: positive, but diminishing marginal support in the supply of purely domestic pollution. It provides environmental policy to redistribute rents between the interest groups.

The political-support function is specified as follows:

$$\max_{V} M = \beta X - V^2,\tag{6.2}$$

where β is the exogenous relative weight of political influence of consumers and labor relative to environmentalists. Consider now the production side. Production needs two inputs, capital K and pollution V. In this model, pollution regulation is not specified in detail and can cover a wide range of environmental problems due to production. It includes water pollution such as sewage released into the river, as well as air pollution caused by sulfur-dioxide emissions. Pollution regulation specifies a maximum allowance of harmful emissions for the producer. Since pollution regulation restricts the use of pollution as 'input of production', regulation adversely affects output. There are two available production technologies. First, there is an old-fashioned and dirty technology H (H for high pollution)

$$X^H = V^{0.9}.$$ (6.3)

For using the H technology and generating output X^H, a given investment K^H has to be undertaken. The second possible technology L (L for low pollution) pollutes the environment less:

$$X^L = A + V^{0.7}.$$ (6.4)

To use the L technology and generate output X^L, a given investment of K^L has to be undertaken.

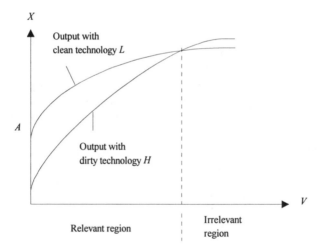

Figure 6.1:   The productivity of the two technologies

As illustrated in Figure 6.1, the clean technology L causes less pollution for any given output than the dirty technology H in the relevant region. The clean technology is more efficient with the use of the environment since it produces a higher output for a given amount of pollution.[5] However, the clean technology is more expensive. For the installation of the production equipment, an investment K^L is necessary, which is higher than the required investment for the dirty technology K^H.

A single import-competing producer in a small, open economy is faced with a given domestic market price $q = q^* + t$, where t is the domestic tariff rate and q^* the world-market price.[6] The producer's profits Π depend on his or her production technology H or L:

$$\Pi^i = qX^i - rK^i, \text{ with } i = H, L. \tag{6.5}$$

The opportunity cost of capital is r. There are two possible types of producers i $= H, L$, who both own the same given capital stock K. Both are able to invest their capital K at home or abroad according to the following two possibilities:

$$\bar{K} = K^H + K^{abroad} \tag{6.6}$$

and

$$\bar{K} = K^L. \tag{6.7}$$

Equation (6.6) shows how capital use is split when the dirty technology is employed. Using K^H for the dirty technology, the remaining capital K^{abroad} is invested abroad and earns a given world market return of r.[7] It is assumed that if capital is not totally used up in the specified production process, the capital is invested abroad since there are no profitable domestic alternatives available. One justification of this assumption is that the sector specificity of capital leaves the producer, who is the only domestic firm in this production sector, only foreign options of investment. In contrast to this, as is shown by equation (6.7), investment in the clean technology needs the complete available capital stock, with the consequence that no investment abroad takes place.

Producer L is the innovative type. He or she is able to choose between both available technologies. If he or she relies on the dirty H technology, he

5   The technology parameter A is assumed to be sufficiently large to ensure that the output of the clean technology is higher than output due to employing the dirty technology for given pollution. This renders the right-hand region of Figure 6.1 irrelevant.

6   The opposite case of an exporter is considered in Section 6.5.

7   Π represents only the profits of the domestic activity; for total profits the opportunity costs of capital use rK have to be added.

or she employs K^H and invests the remaining capital $K^{abroad} = \bar{K} - K^H$ abroad. I assume that parameter A is sufficiently large to make the clean technology superior to the dirty technology. As a consequence, the innovative producer prefers employing the clean technology because profits are higher. Producer H is inflexible and has to stick to the outdated dirty technology H by employing the lesser amount of capital K^H. He or she invests the remaining capital $K^{abroad} = K - K^H$ abroad.

6.2.2 Environmental Policy in a Static Setting under Complete Information

This simple static model with complete information helps to motivate the following. The model is a Stackelberg game where the government sets the pollution limit first and the producer follows by deciding on the allocation of his or her capital. The model is solved by backward induction.

The innovative producer employs the clean L technology because his or her profits are highest with this technology. His or her domestic profits are as follows:

$$\Pi^L = q \cdot X^L - rK^L. \tag{6.8}$$

Substituting equation (6.4) into (6.2), differentiating with respect to V^L, and solving for V^L results in the following politically optimal pollution limit:

$$V^L = (0.35 \cdot \beta)^{\frac{10}{13}}. \tag{6.9}$$

This limit of allowed pollution is higher, the higher β, the political strength of the consumer and labor interests relative to the environmentalists. This can be explained by the policy maker's political-support maximizing via balancing the politically viable interests at the margin. The larger the weight of the consumers and labor in the political process, the more rents can be appropriated by these interests from the environmentalists. Vice versa, the lower the weight β, the more rents can be appropriated by the environmentalists. The tool of this rent-shifting process is pollution regulation.

Now consider the inflexible H type who has to stick to the old-fashioned technology. His or her profits are as follows:

$$\Pi^H = q \cdot X^H - rK^H. \tag{6.10}$$

Substituting (6.3) into (6.2), differentiating with respect to V^H, and solving for V^H results in the politically optimal pollution limit:

$$V^H = (0.45 \cdot \beta)^{\frac{10}{11}}. \tag{6.11}$$

Again the politically optimal pollution limit depends positively on the strength of the consumer and labor interests in the political process. Since producer H relies more heavily on polluting the environment, the politically optimal limit V^H is higher than the limit for the producer with the clean technology V^L.[8] The innovative producer is able to cope with stricter environmental regulation more easily, which enables the government to get support from environmentalists by strict environmental policy without losing much support from labor and consumer interests. The government is less lucky, when confronting the inflexible producer. By providing strict environmental policy to raise support from environmentalists, it faces serious output losses which reduce political support. In this situation, the policy maker will specify a more generous pollution limit.

6.2.3 Environmental Policy in a Static Setting under Incomplete Information

Now consider the case under which the policy maker is uncertain about the type of producer he faces. The policy maker has the belief of p, meaning that he assumes with probability p that he is confronted with the inflexible type H, where $0 < p < 1$. The belief of facing the innovative type is $1 - p$. As explained in Subsection 6.2.2, the policy maker would prefer to set a strict limit if he or she faces the innovative producer, and a generous limit in case of being confronted with the inflexible type. Just as under complete information, the game follows the sequential structure in which the government sets environmental policy first and the producer follows by making his or her input decision. Again the game is solved by backward induction.

Type H sets the out-dated technology K^H because he or she has no other choice. Type L employs the clean technology K^L because the clean technology maximizes his or her profits. Since the risk-neutral policy maker is uncertain, he or she maximizes his or her expected political support which is a linear combination of facing the H type with probability p and of facing the L type with probability $1 - p$:

---

8   This result holds for $\beta > 0.6$, which implies that consumer and labor interests must be of reasonable strength compared to environmental interests.

$$\max_{V} \quad M = p\left[\beta \cdot V^{0,9} - V^2\right] + (1-p)\left[\beta\left(A + V^{0,7}\right) - V^2\right]. \tag{6.12}$$

Differentiating (6.12) with respect to the pollution limit V and solving for V, the result is the politically optimal environmental policy under uncertainty $V(p)$. $V(p)$ is stricter than V^H when facing type H, but less stringent than V^L when facing the innovative producer L. The policy maker chooses a pollution limit, the more restrictive, the higher the probability of facing the innovative type.

The innovative producer benefits from a weak environmental policy, which enables him or her to produce even more and have higher profits. He or she has an interest in the government's belief of him being the H type. Therefore, he or she likes to pretend being the H type to profit from a lower environmental limit. The following section considers how the innovative producer conducts indirect rent seeking which affects the belief of the government, and finally may raise the producer's profits.

6.3 ENVIRONMENTAL POLICY IN A DYNAMIC SETTING UNDER INCOMPLETE INFORMATION

6.3.1 Structure of the Game

The model is expanded to a two-period setting to allow for indirect rent seeking by strategic capital flight of the innovative producer. In the two-period model, both types of producers have to decide in both periods on their investment. The policy maker does not know the ability of the producer to cope with environmental regulation. In the first period, the innovative producer is able to exploit this deficit of knowledge and may deliberately choose the less capital-demanding old-fashioned technology and may invest the remaining capital abroad with the intention of influencing the limit-setting of the policy maker. By investing part of his or her capital abroad, he or she signals his or her difficulties in coping with environmental regulation. The relocation may pay off later in more lenient environmental regulation.

The model structure of Subsection 6.2.3 prevails; there is an inflexible and an innovative producer type. The risk-neutral policy maker has the prior probability p of being confronted with the inflexible type.[9] But unlike in

9   Prior p is the key to solving the game. According to Harsanyi (1967), it is possible to take a game of incomplete information as if it were a game of imperfect but complete information. The type the government faces is decided through a move by nature at the beginning of the game, about which the government has the prior of p.

Subsection 6.2.3, the policy maker is able to learn over time about the producer type and is able to update his or her belief. The possibility of indirect rent seeking by investing abroad arises because the belief of the policy maker can be influenced by the innovative producer.

The timing of the two-period game involves four steps:

1.   In the *first period*, environmental policy is given ($V_1 = \bar{V}$), a simplification which is necessary to concentrate on the pivotal effects. For instance, one can assume that a policy maker just moves into office in the first period and is too late to influence policy making. But he or she is able to observe the first-period investment decision of the producer, which will influence future standard-setting behavior. New and stricter pollution regulation is considered for the second period, a fact that endangers the future profits of the producer.[10]

2.   Next, the producer decides on his or her first-period use of capital and technology. He or she knows about plans to tighten the pollution limit in the second period. Proposed tightening of regulation endangers his or her future profits. The reaction of both possible types of producer is different. The inflexible type has no other option than to stick to the old-fashioned technology by investing K^H. The innovative type has two relevant options. He or she may invest his or her complete capital K by choosing the innovative technology. This strategy maximizes the first-period profits, but reveals his or her identity to the government, which is enabled to strengthen limits in the future. His or her second option is to invest part of the capital K^{abroad} abroad and to mimic the inflexible type by investing in the old-fashioned technology with the remaining capital K^H.

3.   The structure in the *second period* is similar to the Stackelberg game under incomplete information in Subsection 6.2.3. Remember that there is only one producer whose production is regulated. He or she can be either innovative or inflexible, a fact which the policy ma!:er does not know. But in contrast to the belief p of facing the inflexible type in Subsection 6.2.3, the producer is able to influence the policy maker's belief by his or her investment decision in the first period. By observing the producer's capital

---

10   It is a stylized fact in environmental economics that environmental protection rises over time as under a ratchet effect. One can imagine that increasing wealth in society may be the cause for rising demand for environmental amenities and stricter pollution laws. New scientific knowledge about adverse effects of pollution or an environmental accident may trigger new environmental regulation as well.

stock of the first period, the policy maker learns about the type of producer.[11] He or she updates his or her belief and sets the environmental policy V_2 according to this updated, posterior belief.

4. After the policy maker has decided on V_2, the producer chooses his or her second-period investment without strategic ambitions, and the game ends.

Both actors maximize their two-period utilities, the producer his or her two-period profit and the policy maker his or her two-period political support. The policy maker's strategy involves setting V_2 according to his or her information on the type of producer. This information depends on the producer's signal K_1. The innovative producer's strategy consists of two investment decisions K_1 and K_2 which depend on the belief of the policy maker and therefore on the pollution limit V_2. A perfect Bayesian equilibrium is obtained if strategies and beliefs are consistent. Each player's strategy has to be the best response to the other player's strategy, given the beliefs.[12]

6.3.2 Equilibria

Does the innovative producer undertake indirect rent seeking by shifting capital abroad? The final solution depends on the innovative type's costs and benefits of mimicking the inflexible type. The innovative type sacrifices first-period profits if employing the dirty technology and relocating capital abroad. But he or she benefits in the second period due to this indirect rent seeking by obtaining less restrictive pollution regulation.

The innovative type's cost C of mimicking, presented in equation (6.13), is the difference of his or her first-period profits due to the employment of the clean technology and his or her first-period profits from employing the outdated dirty technology.

$$C = \Pi_1(K_1^{L}) - \Pi_1(K_1^{H}) =$$
$$[q(A + \overline{V}^{0,7}) - r \cdot K_1^{L}] - (q \cdot \overline{V}^{0,9} - r \cdot K_1^{H}) > 0. \quad (6.13)$$

---

11 This chapter focuses on the extent of capital relocation because industry flight is central in the public debate. Of course, another possibility of modeling the strategic interaction would be that the policy maker observes the producer's output decision. The size of output rather than the size of capital relocation would become the producer's signal for the policy maker.

12 For detailed conditions for perfect Bayesian equilibria, see Appendix 6A1.

The costs of mimicking are positive by definition: the innovative type does give up first-period profits by employing the dirty technology by relocating capital of K^{abroad} abroad.

The innovative type's mimicking pays off in the second period. The gain due to mimicking $G(\mu)$ is the difference between the innovator's profits in the second period if mimicking was undertaken before, and his or her profits if he or she had revealed him- or herself in the first period.

$$G(\mu)=\Pi_2[K^L{}_2(\mu)]-\Pi_2[K^L{}_2(0)] =$$

$$\underbrace{q[A+V_2(\mu)^{0.7}]-r\cdot K_2{}^L}_{1} - \underbrace{q(A+V_2{}^{L\,0.7})-r\cdot K_2{}^L}_{2} \qquad (6.14)$$

Mimicking causes comparatively low regulation of pollution with high profits in the second period (term 1 of equation (6.14)). On the other hand, by investing in the clean technology in the first period, the innovative producer reveals him- or herself and faces a strict pollution limit with lower profits in the second period (term 2 of equation (6.14)).

Three kinds of perfect Bayesian equilibria are possible.[13]

1.   In a *pooling equilibrium*, strategic relocation takes place. The innovative type mimics the inflexible type by investing K^H and relocating K^{abroad} abroad in the first period. The inflexible type invests K^H in the dirty technology and relocates K^{abroad} in the first period as well. The policy maker is unable to learn from the signal and cannot update its prior p. For that reason the policy maker's posterior belief is $\mu = p$. Equation (6.15) depicts the necessary and sufficient condition for a pooling equilibrium:

$$G(\mu = p) > C. \qquad (6.15)$$

The innovative type's two-period profits due to capital relocation exceed his or her two-period profits from investing in clean technology but suffering from strict pollution regulation.

2.   In a *separating equilibrium*, the innovative type chooses his or her favored clean technology in the first period because the gains due to mimicking do not outweigh the costs. The inflexible producer invests in the

---

13   For existence conditions of the following three perfect Bayesian equilibria, see Appendix 6A2.

dirty technology in the first period. Equation (6.16) depicts the necessary and sufficient condition for a separating equilibrium:

$$G(\mu = 1) < C. \tag{6.16}$$

Mimicking does not pay off for the innovative producer because his or her gains never outweigh the costs of mimicking for any belief of the policy maker. Observing the use of clean technology by the producer in the first period, the policy maker is sure to face the innovative producer ($\mu = 0$). Observing the choice of the dirty technology, the policy maker is sure that the producer is inflexible and therefore sets more lenient environmental regulation ($\mu = 1$). Since the policy maker can accurately identify the firm type by the firm's investment decision in the first period, the policy maker develops two different posterior beliefs ($\mu = 0$ or $\mu = 1$) and sets in the following second period either the strict pollution limit or the generous pollution limit, depending on the actual type of producer.

3.   In the case of *mixed equilibria*, the innovative producer relocates only sometimes, he or she randomizes between the choice of the dirty and the clean technology. Observing the investment K^L in the clean technology, the policy maker is sure to face the innovative type and, consequently, he or she updates p to $\mu = 0$. If the policy maker observes relocation of capital, he or she knows that the inflexible type relocates always and the innovative producer relocates only sometimes. He or she updates p to $p < \mu < 1$ because the probability of facing the inflexible producer is higher than p, because the innovative producer relocates sometimes as well.
     Equation (6.16) depicts the necessary and sufficient condition for mixed equilibria:

$$G(\mu = 1) \ < C < \ G(\mu = p). \tag{6.17}$$

The inflexible type employs the dirty technology in the first period, the innovative type is indifferent between his or her two options dirty and clean and alternates between both. This result is explained as follows: the costs caused by mimicking outweigh the benefits for the innovator (right part of equation (6.17)). For this reason pooling is not profitable. The innovative type would prefer separating. Since $G(\mu = 1) > C$ (left part of equation (6.17)), the policy maker understands that the innovative type has an incentive to deviate from separating, given the policy maker's separating beliefs ($\mu = 1$ if K^H, $\mu = 0$ if K^L in the first period). Therefore, these beliefs are not consistent. The final equilibrium condition for mixed strategies states that the innovative type must be indifferent between both of his or her alternatives:

$$G(\mu = \mu_1) = C, \text{ where } p < \mu_1 < 1. \tag{6.18}$$

The innovative type's gains due to mimicking equal his or her investment in mimicking. The policy maker understands that the innovator alternates between the two alternatives. Remember the prior belief p of facing type H. If the policy maker observes investment in the clean technology, he or she is sure ($\mu = 0$) of being confronted with the innovative type. But if he or she observes investment in the dirty technology, he or she updates p according to Bayes's rule:

$$\mu_1 = \frac{p}{p + x_1(1 - p)}, \text{ where } 0 < x_1 < 1. \tag{6.19}$$

His or her posterior belief μ_1 is higher than p because the innovator does not always mimic. The probability of facing type H increases if observing the choice of the dirty technology. The innovator's probability of mimicking, x_1, induces a posterior belief μ_1 that keeps the innovative type indifferent between the two possible actions. The higher x_1, the closer is the government's posterior belief to his or her pooling belief. The lower x_1, the more certain is the policy maker to face the innovative type.

However, this game is based on the assumption that the policy maker is intelligent: he or she understands the structure of the game and has complete information, except for the type of producer. The results differ if the policy maker is naive: he or she always trusts the output signal in the first period and keeps his or her separating beliefs ($\mu = 1$ if K^H, $\mu = 0$ if K^L) even if the innovator has an incentive to mimic the H type. Since the policy maker is naive, his or her realized political support will be not maximal.

A second case, in which a policy maker does not maximize his or her political support, is the case of a green hard-liner government. This government never believes the producer's signal of being the inflexible one (K^H). It always chooses the strict environmental limit. The policy maker loses political support because he or she neglects the interests of the part of his or her constituency concerned with output and employment.

6.4 RESULTS

6.4.1 The Basic Scenario

Under what circumstances does the innovative producer behave strategically, shifting part of his or her capital abroad? The equilibrium conditions for the pooling equilibrium (6.15) and for the separating equilibrium (6.16) are solved for given parameters.[14] Figure 6.2 depicts the results.

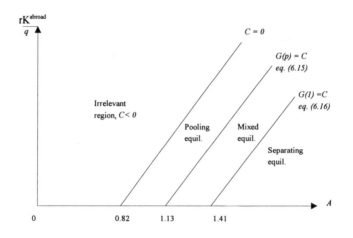

Figure 6.2:   Basic results

A, the parameter indicating the productivity of the innovative technology, is crucial for the equilibrium. A pooling equilibrium is likely if the productivity parameter A is small.[15] In this case, the clean technology's productivity is barely higher than the productivity of the dirty technology. The profits of employing the clean technology are small, and therefore reduce the costs of sacrificing the clean technology. The gains due to mimicking, low pollution regulation, easily outweigh the small costs of mimicking. On the other hand, if the productivity of the clean technology is high, represented through a

---

14   I assume $\beta = 10$ without loss of generality of the argument. The given first-period environmental limit v is chosen to be K^H, a generous limit which the government would prefer to choose if facing the inflexible producer. The prior belief is $p = 0.5$. A variation for β is given in the following subsection.

15   But A has to be large enough so that the innovative producer still gets higher profits from the clean technology than from the dirty technology. The opposite case where the innovator would prefer the dirty technology, graphically represented by the irrelevant region, is ruled out by equation (6.11).

larger parameter value for A, the costs of mimicking increase and profits caused by a low pollution limit do not easily compensate the costs of mimicking. The result is a separating equilibrium, in which the innovative producer always applies the clean technology.

The effects of the size of capital relocation necessary to mimic credibly, rK^{abroad}, on the probability of mimicking, are illustrated in Figure 6.3.[16]

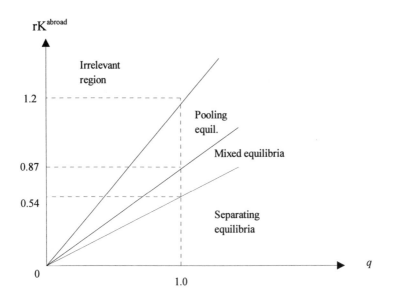

Figure 6.3:   The influence of rK^{abroad} and q on relocation

Mimicking is undertaken by the innovator if the costs of mimicking are low. Mimicking helps the innovator to save capital expenditures if using the dirty technology. The capital not employed if using the dirty technology, K^{abroad}, can be profitably invested abroad, where it earns rK^{abroad}. In contrast to this, all the producer's capital K has to be employed when using the clean technology. If the saved opportunity costs rK^{abroad} are large, the costs of mimicking shrink and make the clean technology less attractive. If, on the other hand, the additional capital expenditures that the clean technology requires are relatively small, mimicking does not pay off. Then, the innovative producer reveals him- or herself and abstains from strategic relocation of his or her capital.

16   For this exercise, the output price q and the value of A is fixed (A = 2).

6.4.2 Low Political Influence of Environmentalists

How does the incidence of strategic relocation depend on the strength of the environmentalists? In this subsection, the weight of the labor and consumer interests β is increased tenfold to $\beta = 100$. Figure 6.4 illustrates this case, in which the political influence of the environmentalists is reduced drastically:

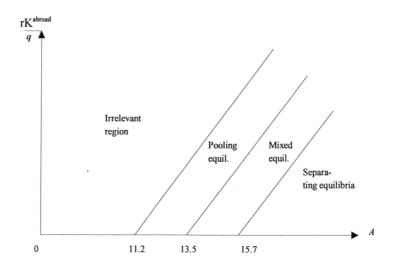

Figure 6.4:   Low political influence of environmentalists

The relative political impact of environmentalists declines, and consequently the politically optimal pollution limit V^L and V^H increases, which can be shown by equations (6.9) and (6.11). One could assume that weak environmental interest groups make strategic capital relocation less likely. Being not influential, so runs the argument, the environmentalists' lobbying for stricter regulation is not successful, environmental regulation is lenient and therefore is not able to endanger producers' profits. Producers would have no reason to shift their capital to pollution havens. But it turns out that the opposite is the case.

For a given A, separating equilibria become more scarce and are replaced by mixed and pooling equilibria (compare Figure 6.4 with Figure 6.2). This can be explained as follows: the dirty technology does relatively better with the expanded pollution limit because this technology is more dependent on the use of the environment. The dirty technology becomes more attractive for the innovative producer, which reduces the cost of mimicking and makes strategic capital relocation more likely. Contrary to intuition, politically weak environmentalists make strategic capital flight more attractive.

6.4.3 Variations of the Prior Belief

What happens if the government has a higher (exogenous) prior probability p of facing the inflexible type? Assume a prior belief of $p = 0.9$. Pooling becomes more attractive for the innovative type, because the government sets a lower environmental standard, the higher its probability of being confronted with the inflexible type. This is demonstrated in Figure 6.5, in which, caused by a higher prior, pooling equilibria replace mixed equilibria. At the extreme of $p = 1$, the government is completely sure that it faces type H. Mixed equilibria cease to exist.

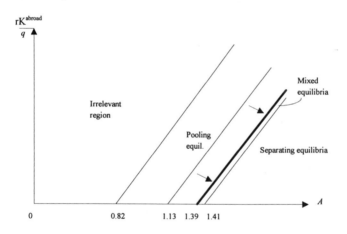

Figure 6.5:   *The case of the prior belief $p = 0.9$*

On the other hand, a small prior belief of $p = 0.1$ makes the government more certain that it faces the innovative type. Hence, it sets a strict pollution standard in the first period. With such a small p, pooling is less attractive for the innovator because mimicking barely reduces the environmental standard. Figure 6.6 illustrates how mixed equilibria replace most pooling equilibria. In the border case of $p = 0$, the policy maker is sure to be confronted with the innovator. If the innovator employs the dirty technology and relocates capital, he or she cannot avoid the situation whereby the strict environmental standard will be chosen. Therefore, pooling equilibria are not profitable and cease to exist.

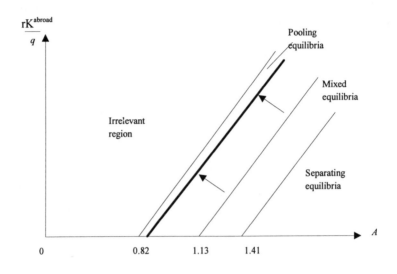

Figure 6.6:   *The case of the prior belief p = 0.1*

The innovative producer relocates capital for strategic reasons if the clean technology is only a little more profitable than the old-fashioned dirty technology. This may happen for two reasons. First, the clean technology requires considerably more capital than the dirty technology. Second, the output price is low so that the productivity gains caused by the new technology do not increase profits considerably.

6.5 TRADE LIBERALIZATION

How does trade liberalization affect environmental regulation and the innovative type's incentive to employ the dirty technology strategically and, in consequence, to relocate capital? The innovator operates in a small, open economy with a given domestic-market price $q = q^* + t$, where q^* is the world-market price and t is the tariff rate. The producer is assumed to compete on the domestic market against foreign rivals. The tariff rate is reduced by trade liberalization, which eases the access of foreign rivals to the home market. Increasing competition drives down the domestic producer price as much as the tariff rate is reduced.

How does trade liberalization affect the costs and benefits of mimicking? A lower output price reduces the costs of imitating the inflexible type because the innovative technology loses some of its lead over the dirty technology.

The profits sacrificed through mimicking are smaller. In the second period, the benefits of less-stringent pollution regulation, obtained by mimicking, decrease as well. However, the costs of mimicking decrease faster than the benefits and, therefore, mimicking becomes more likely. The results are illustrated in Figure 6.7 by an arrow: the removal of the trade barrier shifts part of the equilibria from the separating region to the pooling region.

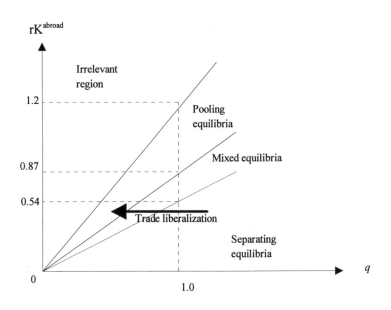

Figure 6.7:   *The effects of trade liberalization: an import-competing*
                producer

Trade liberalization hurts the import-competing producer through a reduction of his or her market price. Strategic relocation is his or her tool to recapture part of the losses. Environmental regulation serves as an instrument of compensation which the producer seeks to influence by indirect rent seeking: he or she chooses the dirty technology and deliberately relocates capital. The probability of strategic relocation increases under trade liberalization because the producer, adversely affected by a decline in his or her output price, can now deceive the government in his or her ability to cope with environmental regulation more easily. By relocating part of his or her capital abroad, the producer deceives the policy maker about his or her dependence on the dirty technology and, therefore, on lenient environmental regulation.

The results are bleak for the environment, but depend on the assumption of the producer being import competitive. Figure 6.8 illustrates how the results alter if the producer is an exporter who gains from global trade liberalization. His or her given domestic-market price is $q = q^* - t^*$, where q^* is the world market price and t^* the world tariff rate.[17] This, for instance, is the case of trade liberalization due to multilateral trade negotiations in the WTO framework in which worldwide tariffs in a wide range of goods are expected to fall.

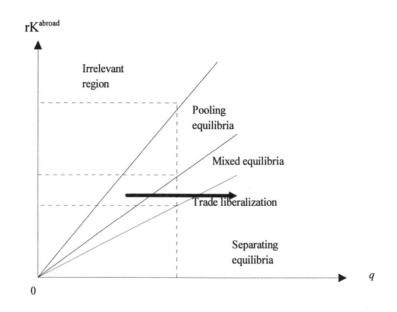

Figure 6.8:   Foreign trade liberalization: an exporting producer

A lower foreign tariff rate provides additional opportunities in export markets for the producer and, hence, increase his or her output price. The costs of mimicking rise while the gains due to mimicking rise as well. Since the costs of mimicking increase faster than the benefits, mimicking is now less likely if the producer is exposed to free trade.

17   Again, the country in consideration is a small open economy which is not able to influence world-market prices. Therefore, a fall of the world tariff rate increases the producer price.

6.6 CONCLUSIONS

This chapter has illustrated that an entrepreneur may relocate production for strategic reasons rather than because of a real loss of competitiveness if he or she is expecting a tightening of environmental regulation in the future. Capital flight is intended to signal damage to the policy maker due to increasing environmental control that might or might not occur in reality. Capital flight for strategic reasons is possible because the government is uncertain about the producer's ability to adapt to environmental regulation. Inasmuch as foreign direct investment is motivated by this signaling intention, politicians should not be concerned; on the contrary, their responsiveness to such 'threats' would tend to increase rather than reduce the export of capital. Several results are obtained.

The producer's costs of indirect rent seeking are the profits sacrificed by applying the less profitable technology. His or her costs are low if the replacement of his or her preferred clean technology by the dirty technology causes only a small decline in profits. Sacrificing the clean technology is easier, the more capital is saved when applying the dirty technology. Since the capital saved can be profitably invested abroad, strategic capital flight raises total profits. Contrary to intuition, the probability of strategic capital flight taking place increases with the size of capital flight necessary to credibly show to the policy maker injury due to strict environmental regulation.

Trade liberalization increases the probability of strategic relocation of an import-competing firm. Since trade liberalization intensifies competition, the firm loses market share to its foreign competitors. Already hit by liberalization, the costs of sacrificing his or her preferred clean technology are lower, making strategic capital flight cheaper. With free trade, it is easier for the firm to deceive the government in his or her ability to cope with environmental regulation by relocating part of his or her capital abroad.

One might assume that strong environmental interest groups make strategic capital relocation more profitable because their lobbying for stricter regulation endangers producers' profits. However, this is not the case. Stronger environmentalists raise the costs of strategic ambitions by making the dirty technology which is necessary for mimicking less attractive compared to the other technology available. Therefore, strong environmental interest groups help to avoid strategic relocation.

APPENDIX 6A1:   CONDITIONS FOR A PERFECT
BAYESIAN EQUILIBRIUM

A perfect Bayesian equilibrium is obtained if the innovative type's strategy
(K_1 , K_2), the government's strategy V_2 , the beliefs p (prior) and μ
(posterior) satisfy the following requirements:

1. K_2 maximizes the profit in the second period. The choice of K_2 has no
     strategic component because the game ends with the setting of K_2 .
2. V_2 maximizes the expected value of the political support in the second
     period which depends on the posterior belief μ and on the investment
     decision in the second period K_2 .
3. K_1 maximizes the two-period profit of the innovative producer type,
     given the second-period strategies.
4.   The posterior belief μ is Bayes consistent with the prior belief p and with
     the firm's first-period strategy K_1 .

APPENDIX 6A2:   EXISTENCE CONDITIONS FOR THE
EQUILIBRIA

For the existence of a *pooling equilibrium*, the out-of-equilibrium beliefs and
actions have to be specified. The innovative type could play his first-period
optimal strategy, but has no incentive because the gains due to mimicking
exceed the losses. The policy maker could hold the out-of-equilibrium belief
$\mu = 1$, being sure to be confronted with the inflexible type. But he or she
knows that both types set K^H . Under the policy maker's belief $\mu = 1$ the
pollution limit would be too lenient to maximize his or her expected political
support because there is a change in the probability of facing the innovative
type. Therefore, holding the prior belief p is the policy maker's optimal
choice.

What out-of-equilibrium actions and beliefs do we have to consider for the
existence of a *separating equilibrium*? Since pooling is not profitable, the
innovative type chooses the clean technology in the first period. The policy
maker could hold the out-of-equilibrium belief of $\mu = 0$ if observing this
technology choice. But because of (6.16), the innovative type has no
incentive to mimic the H type. Only type H employs the dirty technology.
Therefore, the beliefs $\mu = 0$ if observing the clean technology, and $\mu = 1$ if
observing the dirty technology, are consistent.

7 Comparison of Results and Policy Recommendations

7.1 COMPARISON OF RESULTS

The ongoing process of economic integration has caused a debate about whether trade liberalization causes a deterioration in the environment. This debate, however, has assumed that environmental policy is not altered by free trade; it has failed to recognize crucial effects of changes in environmental policy due to free trade. NAFTA, for instance, has led to tighter environmental regulation. The Environmental Side Agreement and the Environmental Border Plan are linked to NAFTA and provide the institutional framework for a better environment. A second example is the European Common Market, in which integration induced a significant increase of environmental regulation on the Community level, a condition for higher environmental quality especially in the south of Europe.

The effects of free trade on environmental policy are the hole to be filled with this book, since these crucial effects have so far been largely unexplored. Two bodies of literature have been merged for this purpose. First, there is the literature on the environmental effects of trade, which explores the environmental effects of changes in the scale and composition of economic activity due to free trade. Second, the political-economic approach is applied to environmental policy making. Environmental policy is determined in an institutional setting in which self-interested policy makers confront the relevant interest groups who gain or lose from the politicians' regulation. As economic integration alters the groups' stakes, their lobbying activities with respect to environmental policy change and, therefore, alter environmental policy as well.

Consequently, the group interests with regard to environmental policy needed to be investigated. While the interest of environmentalists is obvious – they favor strict pollution regulation – it turned out that the interests of producers are not so clear-cut. As one would expect, producers often oppose strict environmental regulation since stricter standards cause losses. When producers lose from economic integration as well, lenient environmental policy may serve as a policy instrument to compensate them for their losses.

Hence, the policy maker who is confronted with the demand for compensation of the losing industry, may be tempted to reduce pollution standards or to refrain from an increase of environmental control.

However, there are instances in which environmental regulation increases producers' profits. This is the case if there is competition between different types of producers, while some producers depend on polluting the environment to a lesser extent than others do (clean versus dirty producers). Therefore, by increasing the compliance cost of the dirty producers, strict regulation may improve the competitiveness of the clean producers. If these clean producers lose from economic integration, the policy maker may choose a stricter standard to compensate them.

Table 7.1 illustrates how the impact of trade policies and environmental regulation on producers' profits has determined the results of this book.

Chapter 4 demonstrated that in a two-sector open-economy model with perfect competition the effects of economic integration on environmental policy depend on which sector of production is gaining and which one is losing from free trade. If the dirty sector of production is import competing and, hence, loses from free trade, this sector is compensated by a more lenient environmental policy. Consequently, part of the gains from free trade, occurring in the exporting clean sector, are redistributed by more lenient pollution regulation to the loser from free trade, the dirty sector. Here, the general-equilibrium effects of environmental policy are crucial: the clean sector of production, even though not directly affected by environmental regulation, loses from more lenient regulation. More lenient regulation raises the productivity of capital in the dirty sector, attracts labor from the clean sector and increases profits in the dirty sector while lowering profits in the clean sector.

However, the endogenous environmental policy reaction can also drive up pollution standards. If the clean sector loses from integration, the gains from free trade are redistributed from the dirty to the clean sector by more stringent environmental regulation. This applies to the case of the US in the course of trade liberalization agreed upon in NAFTA. An empirical analysis of the US trade structure has shown that the US specializes in comparably dirty production, a specialization which was found to be reinforced by the NAFTA agreement. As NAFTA increases the export opportunities of dirty US industries, the clean industries lose and, consequently, are being compensated by the tightening of environmental control. Hence, the endogenous reaction of environmental policy caused by NAFTA improves the environment in the US.

In the two-country model with imperfect competition of producers, portrayed in Chapter 5, I focus again on the gainers and the losers from economic integration. Since countries are large, environmental policy making in one country influences decisions with regard to the environment in the other country. Although the producer in one country gains by free trade because of better access to the foreign market, some of his or her gains are

Table 7.1: Overview of the results

Effects of economic integration ($dt < 0$)	The dirty producer is losing from integration	The dirty producer is gaining from integration	Endogenous environmental policy mechanism
Model set-up			
Perfect competition in a two-sector model (Chapter 4)	Pollution (V) increases: $dV / dt < 0$	Pollution (V) decreases: $dV / dt > 0$	If the dirty producer loses from integration, he or she is compensated by lenient regulation; if the clean producer loses from integration, he or she is compensated by strict regulation.
Imperfect competition in a two-country model (Chapter 5)	The pollution standard (v) decreases: $dv / dt < 0$	The pollution standard (v) increases: $dv / dt > 0$	The dirty loser in country 1 is compensated with a more lenient pollution standard v. The dirty winner in country 2 is burdened with a stricter standard.
Imperfect competition and imperfect information in a one-country- and one-sector model (Chapter 6)	Pollution increases: $dV / dt < 0$	Pollution decreases: $dV / dt > 0$	If the producer loses, the probability of strategic relocation increases and, consequently, pollution regulation V becomes more lenient. If the producer gains, regulation becomes stricter.

redistributed by the policy maker to the environmentalists, who suffer from a deteriorating environment as production expands. A stricter pollution standard is the means of compensation for the environmentalists. In the second country, the producer loses from free trade because competition of the foreign producer becomes more intense. The home producer is compensated by a more lenient environmental standard. Part of the environmentalists' gains, an improved environment caused by declining home production, are redistributed to the producer. Since economic integration creates gainers and losers, Chapter 5 found that one country raises its pollution standard, whereas the other country lowers its standard.

However, results become more clear-cut if European integration is considered. Taking the institutional set-up of the European Union into account, the possibility arises that both countries (or country groups) drive up their pollution standards. If economic integration causes a convergence of the economies, a case which is likely for the European Union, I show that convergence is the precondition for a common environmental policy with stricter pollution standards. This result is driven by the ability of policy makers to cooperate in standard setting, avoiding strategic interaction which causes the downward competition of environmental regulation. The emergence of a common European environmental policy, where pollution regulation is largely transferred from the single member states to Brussels, suggests that this case holds for the EU.

A final issue, addressed in Chapter 6, analyzes the often voiced fear that economic integration could induce producers to relocate to low-standard countries and thereby pressure policy makers to relax home environmental standards. Hence, integration could cause a deterioration in the environment by lowering environmental standards. Chapter 6 shows that firms may indeed have the incentive to relocate for environmental-policy reasons, but relocation may not be caused by producers having real difficulties in complying with strict regulation. It is shown that producers relocate their facilities abroad for strategic reasons: relocation is the producers' tool of indirect rent seeking to convince the policy maker to relax standards.

The effects of economic integration on such strategic behavior depend – as in the previous chapters – on the effects of free trade on the firms involved. If firms lose from free trade, their incentives to behave strategically increase since the productivity of investing capital at home declines. Therefore, the costs of strategic relocation decrease and make strategic relocation more likely. If the firms gain from free trade, their incentive to relocate for strategic reasons declines, since the productivity of employing capital at home increases.

The conciliatory results of this inquiry are based on the endogenous reaction of environmental policy. Even if economic integration puts a strain on the natural environment – which is by no means certain – the endogenous reaction of environmental policy may contribute to a mitigation of the adverse effects. Therefore, neither unilateral eco-dumping nor a rat-race of a downward competition of standards are expected to take place. This is the major result from the investigation of the environmental consequences of NAFTA in Chapter 4 and the European Common Market in Chapter 5. Chapter 6 goes a step further. Even if we observe adverse producer reactions, apparently induced by strict environmental regulation, the underlying reason may be purely strategic. If producers have higher incentives to relocate facilities just for strategic reasons when trade is liberalized, there is no necessity for policy makers to relax pollution standards. Hence, apparently simple truths, for example, that economic integration changes the composition of the economy toward a more pollution-intensive production or that the downward competition of environmental standards may cause a deterioration in the environment, need not hold.

However, positive environmental effects of free trade do take place, at least partly, for non-environmental reasons. Environmentalism poses opportunities to raise trade protection directly or indirectly by using environmental standards, which pose barriers to entry for foreign firms. Therefore, free trade may be beneficial to the environment, but in part for protectionist reasons. This is particularly relevant for environmental product standards since they may raise the cost of compliance for foreign firms in the manner of 'raising rivals' cost'. Because this book is concerned mainly with production standards, the issue of product standards is left for future exploration.

A second issue, where future research from a political-economic perspective is advised, is the case of social and labor standards. Recently, regulations such as environmental standards have become popular as attempts to limit free trade. In particular, developing countries are requested to introduce regulations for working-place safety or against child labor, if they want to avoid the risk of trade protection. The underlying reason is that labor-intensive industries in developed countries have considerable interests in limiting the market access of products from low-wage countries. Hence, the accusation of 'social dumping' toward developing countries is an attempt to restrict competition, comparable with the accusation of 'environmental dumping'. Furthermore, social protection, like environmental protection, qualifies for politically successful coalitions of producers with 'purer' interests – public interest groups on social issues, for instance.

7.2 POLICY RECOMMENDATIONS

Economists usually recommend that trade and environment policies should not be intermingled. In particular, trade policies should not be applied to solve environmental problems since trade policies cannot, or only at high cost, solve environmental problems. Efficient solutions require tackling environmental problems at their source and at the lowest cost possible. Hence, environmental policies, not trade policies, are required to solve environmental problems. In particular, environmental policies, which rely on market-based instruments of pollution regulation, need to be selected.

Although the above policy recommendations are valuable, in reality they are rarely applied. There are numerous inefficient environmental regulations and many attempts to limit free trade for environmental reasons. In Section 2.3, the political economy of trade and the environment illustrated the reasons for this puzzle. The underlying cause – and this is emphasized through the whole book – is that policy making, not only in the field of trade and the environment, is determined by self-interested political agents. Are there opportunities to remove environmental regulation from the selfish demands of interests groups and politicians? What has to be done to obtain policy results which are akin to the above recommendations?[1]

The harmonization of environmental regulation could mitigate pressures on single governments to lower standards as environmental policy becomes an attractive substitute for trade policy. With regard to European integration, Chapter 5 shows that the harmonization of environmental *production standards* between countries could be helpful to avoid a possible downward competition of standards. Furthermore, with regard to environmental *product standards*, Runge (1990) advises harmonization to avoid eco-protectionism since countries may choose stricter than efficient product standards to keep foreign producers off the domestic market.

However, there are two arguments against harmonization. First, there are efficiency losses from harmonization. As discussed in Section 2.1, countries have different assimilative capacities with regard to the environment and differ in the valuation of environmental goods and services. Hence, in general, efficiency requires that countries select standards independently.[2] The second argument relates to the objectives of the agents involved in the harmonization of environmental policy. Producers of high-standard countries may favor high-level harmonization with the intention of limiting competition of producers from countries with lower standards. Producers from high-standard countries often accuse their foreign competitors of eco-dumping, that is, of having an 'unjust' competitive advantage caused by lower environmental standards. In the political discussion, the term 'level playing field' is frequently used by such producer interests to demand the

---

1   Since trade policies have been considered exogenous in this study, the question regarding better trade policies will not be answered here. For a survey on trade policy advice from a political-economy point of view, see Schuknecht (1992, Chapter 10).

2   The need to cooperate is higher if pollution is transboundary since the problem of free-riding, typical for the provision of international public goods, arises.

harmonization of standards. Therefore, a trade-off exists. On the one hand, harmonization is beneficial because it limits the political competition which may be responsible for inefficiently lenient environmental standards. On the other hand, the harmonization of standards causes efficiency losses, since level-playing-field arguments are used with the intention of limiting economic competition.

A second and more promising approach to reduce the influence of (protectionist) interests on environmental policy is the compensation of the losers of free trade. This is particularly relevant for environmentalists who may side with protectionists in their opposition to economic integration. Therefore, policy-induced environmental improvements as a part of economic integration may limit opposition to free trade to the (real) protectionists. The Environmental Side Agreement and the Border Plan of NAFTA serve as an example of a compensation strategy. Neither measures eliminated the environmentalists' protest against NAFTA, but may have helped to mitigate their opposition. Similarly, the World Trade Organization established a Committee on Trade and Environment to include environmental concerns into trade policy making. The WTO is inviting environmentalists to participate in the discussion of trade and environment issues. For instance, environmentalists joined the first WTO ministerial meeting in Singapore, December 9–13, 1996.[3] Such cooperation could limit green opposition to free trade as well.

A further suggestion for the improvement of environmental policy making is decision making on a constitutional level. Staehelin-Witt and Blöchliger (1990) suggest the creation of an 'environmental central bank' in which experts from important groups of society determine environmental regulation. They hope that an independent environmental central bank will remove environmental decision making from the short-term pressures of day-to-day politics and will help to focus policy making on the long-term character of many environmental problems.

However, this approach has considerable shortcomings. If environmental policy making is not accessible to interest groups, other policies may become more attractive for them. If environmentalists lose power to influence environmental policies directly, they may choose a more indirect way of lobbying the environment by siding protectionist interests via lobbying for protection and reduced output, for instance. Or, to take another example, producers may replace their lobbying on environmental issues with lobbying on labor issues. The developing debate on wage dumping or social dumping points in this direction. In sum, if environmental policy making is removed

---

3   For upcoming trade and environment issues within the WTO, see Whalley (1996).

from day-to-day politics, other policy issues need to be removed from day-to-day politics as well.

A second shortcoming of the central bank proposal relates to principal–agent problems in such an 'independent' institution. How do we ensure that the self-interested officials in this organization select the appropriate policies? There are two problems to be solved: the selection of the environmental objective and the control of the execution of the selected objective by the environmental central bank. Both are difficult to achieve. A comprehensive agreement within society on a global environmental objective is scarcely possible since environmental policy covers many different aspects. Without a clear objective, the control of environmental policy making is extremely difficult as well. In contrast to this, the definition of a monetary policy objective, to be adhered to by an ordinary central bank, is easier. Often, there is a broad agreement within society about which objective, a certain rate of inflation, should be achieved. Moreover, the control is not difficult since the result of monetary policy can be measured relatively easily.

The third problem of the central bank proposal concerns the implementation of policy making by an environmental central bank. In contrast to monetary policy, environmental policy is intertwined basically with every other issue of policy making. Environmental policy making, which is undertaken independently, neglects the necessary coordination between environmental regulation and other policy issues. Independent environmental policy making poses severe limits to policy making in general.

However, the idea of an environmental central bank points in a positive direction. The introduction of forces which strengthen good environmental policy making could reduce the distortions of the political process. For instance, environmental policy review institutions could provide cost–benefit analysis of potential and actual policy measures. If such institutions are supplied with the power to present their suggestions to a wider public, at least some information problems of voters could be mitigated. This could help to reduce rational ignorance of voters and, thereby, limit the influence of interest groups. For example, in Germany, a body of experts from different sciences advises the German government on environmental policy. However, the impact of this body is limited because it is not independent from the government and its main task is only to publish an annual environmental report.[4]

---

4   This body is called *Rat der Sachverständigen für Umwelfragen*.

Bibliography

Amelung, T. and M. Diehl (1991), 'Deforestation of Tropical Rainforests: Economic Causes and Impact on Development', *Kieler Studien*, **241**, Tübingen, Mohr.

Anderson, K. (1992a), 'Agricultural Trade Liberalization and the Environment: A Global Perspective', *World Economy*, **15**, 153–71.

Anderson, K. (1992b), 'Effects on the Environment and Welfare of Liberalizing World Trade: The Cases of Coal and Food', in: Anderson and Blackhurst (eds) (1992), 145–72.

Anderson, K. (1993), 'Economic Growth, Environmental Issues and Trade', in C.F. Bergsten and M. Noland (eds), *Pacific Dynamism and the International Economic System*, Washington, DC, Institute for International Economics, 341–63.

Anderson, K. and R. Blackhurst (eds) (1992), *The Greening of World Trade Issues*, New York, Harvester Wheatsheaf.

Barbier, E. (1994), 'The Environmental Effects of Trade in the Forestry Sector', in OECD (1994), 55–102.

Barbier, E., B. Burgess, T. Swanson and D. Pearce (1990), *Elephants, Economics and Ivory*, London, Earthscan.

Barrett, S. (1994), 'Strategic Environmental Policy and International Trade', *Journal of Public Economics*, **54**, 325–38.

Bartik, T. (1988), 'The Effects of Environmental Regulation on Business Location in the United States', *Growth and Change*, **19**, 22–44.

Bernholz, P. and F. Breyer (1993), *Grundlagen der Politischen Ökonomie*, Vol. 1, Tübingen, J.C.B. Mohr/Siebeck.

Bernholz, P. and F. Breyer (1994), *Grundlagen der Politischen Ökonomie*, Vol. 2, Tübingen, J.C.B. Mohr/Siebeck.

Bindseil, U. and C. Hantke (1997), 'The Power Distribution in Decision Making among EU Member States', *European Journal of Political Economy*, **13**, 171–85.

Birdsall, N. and D. Wheeler (1992), 'Trade Policy and Industrial Pollution in Latin America: Where are the Pollution Havens?', in Low (ed.) (1992a), 159–68.

Bommer, R. (1996a), *Trade, Environment and Development, Lessons from Empirical Studies: The Case of Thailand*, Preliminary Synthesis Report, Trade and Environment Board, Geneva, UNCTAD.

Bommer, R. (1996b), 'Das Drei-Liter-Auto – ein sinnvoller Lösungsansatz?', *Wirtschaftsdienst*, **76**, 256–60.

Bommer, R. (1996c), 'Environmental Regulation of Production Processes in the European Union: A Political-Economy Approach', *Aussenwirtschaft*, **51**, 559–82.

Bommer, R. (1998), 'Environmental Policy and Industrial Competitiveness: The Pollution-Haven Hypothesis Reconsidered', *Review of International Economics*, forthcoming.

Bommer, R. and G.G. Schulze (1994), 'Economic Integration and Environmental Policy: Does NAFTA Increase Pollution?', Working Paper Series II, No. 218, University of Konstanz, Department of Economics.

Braga, C. (1992), 'Tropical Forests and Trade Policy: The Cases of Indonesia and Brazil', in: Low (ed.) (1992a), 173–94.

Brander, J. and B. Spencer (1985), 'Export Subsidies and International Market Share Rivalry', *Journal of International Economics*, **18**, 83–100.

Brown, D., A. Deardorff and R. Stern (1992a), 'A North American Free Trade Agreement: Analytical Issues and a Computational Assessment', *World Economy*, **15**, 11–29.

Brown, D., A. Deardorff and R. Stern (1992b), 'North American Integration', *Economic Journal*, **102**, 1507–18.

Buchanan, J. and G. Tullock (1975), 'Polluters' Profits and Political Response: Direct Control Versus Taxes', *American Economic Review*, **65**, 139–47.

Burgess, J. (1990), 'The Contribution of Efficient Energy Pricing to Reducing Carbon Dioxide Emissions', *Energy Policy*, **18**, 449–55.

Burgess, J. (1991), 'Environmental Effects of Trade in Endangered Species and Biodiversity', Paper Prepared for the Joint Session of Trade and Environment Experts, Paris, OECD.

Cadot, O. and B. Sinclair-Desgagné (1995), 'Environmental Standards and Industrial Policy', *Journal of Environmental Economics and Management*, **29**, 228–37.

Carraro, C. (ed.) (1994), *Trade, Innovation, Environment*, Dordrecht, Kluwer.

Chichilnisky, G. (1994), 'North–South Trade and the Global Environment', *American Economic Review*, **84**, 851–74.

Conrad, K. (1996a), 'Optimal Environmental Policy for Oligopolistic Industries under Intra-Industry Trade', in C. Carraro, Y. Katsoulacos and A. Xepapadeux (eds), *Environmental Policy and Market Structure*, Amsterdam, Kluwer, 65–83.

Conrad, K. (1996b), 'Choosing Emission Taxes under International Price Competition', in: C. Carraro, Y. Katsoulacos and A. Xepapadeux (eds), *Environmental Policy and Market Structure*, Amsterdam, Kluwer.

Copeland, B. and M. Taylor (1994), 'North–South Trade and the Environment', *Quarterly Journal of Economics*, **109**, 755–87.

Copeland, B. and M. Taylor (1995), 'Trade and Transboundary Pollution', *American Economic Review*, **85**, 716–37.

Cromwell, C. and J. Winpenny (1991), *Has Economic Reform Harmed the Environment? A Review of Structural Adjustment in Malawi*, London, Overseas Development Institute.

Cropper, M. and W. Oates (1992), 'Environmental Economics: A Survey', *Journal of Economic Literature*, **30**, 675–740.

Cruz, W. and R. Repetto (1993), 'The Environmental Effects of Stabilization and Structural Adjustment Programs: The Philippines Case', Washington, DC, World Resources Institute.

Daly, H. (1994), 'Die Gefahren des freien Handels', *Spektrum der Wissenschaft*, January, 40–46.

Daly, H. and R. Goodland (1994), 'An Ecological–Economic Assessment of Deregulation of International Commerce under GATT', *Ecological Economics*, **9**, 73–92.

Dean, J. (1992), 'Trade and Environment: A Survey of the Literature', in: Low (ed.) (1992a), 15–28.

Dewees, D. (1983), 'Instrument Choice in Environmental Policy', *Economic Inquiry*, **21**, 53–71.

Dohlman, E. (1990), 'The Trade Effects of Environmental Regulation', *OECD Observer*, **162**, 28–32.

Economist, The (1993), 'Mexican Butterflies', July 10, 47.

Economist, The (1996), 'The Discreet Charm of Provincial Asia', April 27, 69–70.

Esty, D. (1994a), *Greening the GATT*, Washington, DC, Institute for International Economics.

Esty, D. (1994b), 'Making Trade and Environmental Policies Work Together: Lessons from NAFTA', *Aussenwirtschaft*, **49**, 59–79.

European Commission (1988), 'The Economics of 1992', *European Economy*, **35**.

Faure, M. and J. Lefevere (1994), 'Some Public Interest and Private Interest Aspects of Environmental Standard Setting in Europe', Paper presented at the Annual Conference of the European Public Choice Society, Valencia, April, 6–8.

Forster, B. (1981), 'Environmental Regulation and the Distribution of Income in Simple General Equilibrium Models', in: M. Ballabon (ed.), *Economic Perspectives*, New York, Harwood, 105–29.

French, H. (1993), 'Costly Tradeoffs: Reconciling Trade and the Environment', Worldwatch Paper No. 113, Washington, DC, Worldwatch.

Frey, R.L., E. Staehelin-Witt and H. Blöchlinger (1991): *Mit Oekonomie zur Oekonomie: Analyse und Lösungen des Umweltproblems aus ökonomischer Sicht*, Basel, Helbing & Lichtenhahn.

GATT (1993a), 'Trade and Environmental Group Examines Transparency of Trade-related Environmental Measures as well as Labeling and Packaging Issues', *Trade and Environment*, **1**, News and Views from GATT, Occasional Bulletin, April 1, Geneva, General Agreement on Tariffs and Trade.

GATT (1993b), 'Trade Provisions Contained in Multilateral Environmental Agreements', Note by the Secretariat, TRE/W/1/Rev.1, Geneva, General Agreement on Tariffs and Trade.

GATT (1994), 'The Results of the Uruguay Round of Multilateral Trade Negotiations', Geneva, General Agreement of Tariffs and Trade.

Globerman, S. (1993), 'Trade Liberalization and the Environment', in: S. Globerman and M. Walker (eds), *Assessing NAFTA: A Trinational Analysis*, Vancouver, Fraser Institute, 292–314.

Grasstek, C. van (1992), 'The Political Economy of Trade and the Environment in the US', in: Low (ed.) (1992a), 227–44.

Gray, H. and I. Walter (1983), 'Investment-related Trade Distortions in Petrochemicals', *Journal of World Trade Law*, **17**, 283–307.

Grossman, G. (1995), 'Pollution and Growth: What Do We Know?', in: I. Goldin and A. Winters (eds), *The Economics of Sustainable Development*, New York, Cambridge University Press, 19–46.

Grossman, G. and E. Helpman (1994), 'Protection for Sale', *American Economic Review*, **84**, 833–50.

Grossman, G. and A. Krueger (1993), 'Environmental Impacts of a North American Free Trade Agreement', in: P. Garber (ed.), *The US–Mexico Free Trade Agreement*, Cambridge, MA, MIT Press.

Grossman, G. and Krueger, A. (1995), 'Economic Growth and the Environment', *Quarterly Journal of Economics*, **60**, 353–77.

Hahn, R. (1990), 'The Political Economy of Environmental Regulation: Towards a Unifying Framework', *Public Choice*, **65**, 21–47.

Hardin, G. (1968), 'The Tragedy of the Commons', *Science*, **162**, 1243–8.

Harsanyi, J. (1967), 'Games with Incomplete Information Played by Bayesian Players, Parts I, II and III', *Management Science*, **14**, 159–82, 320–34, 486–502.

Helpman, E. and P. Krugman (1989), *Trade Policy and Market Structure'*, Cambridge, MA, MIT Press.

Hillman, A. (1989, Second Printing 1994), *The Political Economy of Protection*, Chur, Harwood Academic Publishers.

Hillman, A. (1982), 'Declining Industries and Political-support Protectionist Motives', *American Economic Review*, **72**, 1180–87.

Hillman, A. and C. Bullard III (1978), 'Energy, the Heckscher–Ohlin Theorem, and U.S. International Trade', *American Economic Review*, **68**, 96–106.

Hillman, A. and P. Moser (1996), 'Trade Liberalization as Politically Optimal Exchange of Market Access', in: M. Canzoneri, W. Ethier and V. Grilli (eds), *The New Transatlantic Economy*, New York, Cambridge University Press, 295–312.

Hillman, A. and H.W. Ursprung (1988), 'Domestic Politics, Foreign Interests and International Trade Policy', *American Economic Review*, **78**, 729–45.

Hillman, A. and H.W. Ursprung (1992), 'The Influence of Environmental Concerns on the Political Determination of Trade Policy', in: Anderson and Blackhurst (eds) (1992), 193–220.

Hillman, A. and H.W. Ursprung (1994), 'Greens, Supergreens, and International Trade Policy: Environmental Concerns and Protectionism', in: Carraro (ed.) (1994), 75–108.

Holtz-Eakin, D. and T. Selden (1992), 'Stocking the Fires? CO_2–Emissions and Economic Growth', NBER Working Paper No. 4248, Cambridge, MA, National Bureau of Economic Research.

Hufbauer, G. and J. Schott (1992), *North American Free Trade: Issues and Recommendations*, Washington, DC: Institute for International Economics.

Hughes, G. (1990), 'Are the Costs of Cleaning up Eastern Europe Exaggerated? Economic Reform and the Environment', CEPR Discussion Paper No. 482, London.

IMF (1994), 'International Trade Policies – The Uruguay Round and Beyond', Volume II, Background Papers, World Economic and Financial Surveys, Washington, DC, International Monetary Fund.

International Environmental Reporter (1996a), 'Officials Expected in May to Approve Plan for Environmental Infrastructure', April 3, 267.

International Environmental Reporter (1996b), 'Mexican, US Officials Reach Accord on Plan to Create Binational Pollution Zone', April 3, 293.

Jaffe, A., S. Peterson, P. Portney and R. Stavins (1995), 'Environmental Regulation and the Competitiveness of US Manufacturing: What Does the Evidence Tell Us?', *Journal of Economic Literature*, **33**, 132–63.

Johnson, H. (1953/54), 'Optimum Tariffs and Retaliation', *Review of Economic Studies*, **21**, 142–53.

Jones, R. (1971), 'A Three-Factor Model in Theory, Trade and History', in: J. Bhagwati et al. (eds), *Trade, Balance of Payments and Growth*, Papers on International Economics in Honor of Charles Kindleberger, Amsterdam, North-Holland, 3–21.

Jorgenson, D. and M.S. Ho (1993), *Trade Policy and US Economic Growth*, Cambridge, MA, Harvard Institute of Economic Research.

Kalt, J. (1988), 'The Impact of Domestic Environmental Regulatory Policies on US International Competitiveness', in: M. Spence and H. Hazard (eds), *International Competitiveness*, Cambridge, MA, Harper & Row, 221–62.

Kennedy, P. (1994), 'Equilibrium Pollution Taxes in Open Economies with Imperfect Competition', *Journal of Environmental Economics and Management*, **27**, 49–63.

Kirchgässner, G. (1992), 'Ansatzmöglichkeiten zur Lösung Europäischer Umweltprobleme', *Aussenwirtschaft*, **47**, 55–77.

Kirchgässner, G. and E. Mohr (1996), 'Trade Restrictions as Viable Means of Enforcing Compliance with International Environmental Law: An Economic Assessment', in: R. Wolfrum (ed.), *Enforcing Environmental Standards: Economic Mechanisms as Viable Means?*, Berlin, Springer, 199–226.

Klepper, G. (1992), 'The Political Economy of Trade and the Environment in Western Europe', in: Low (ed.) (1992a), 247–60.

Körber, A. (1997), 'Raising Rivals' Costs with Environmental Regulation – An Intertemporal Lobbying Approach', University of Konstanz, Department of Economics, manuscript.

Krägenow, T. (1996), 'Umweltkiller EU', *Greenpeace Magazin*, 4/1996, 10–15.

Krugman, P. (1987), 'Is Free Trade Passé?', *Journal of Economic Perspectives*, **1**, 131–44.

Krugman, P. (1991), *Geography and Trade*, Cambridge, MA, MIT Press.

Krutilla, K. (1991), 'Environmental Regulation in an Open Economy', *Journal of Environmental Economics and Management*, **20**, 127–42.

Landis Gabel, H. (1992), 'Trade Liberalization, Transportation, and the Environment', *Energy Journal*, **13**, 185–206.

Landis Gabel, H. (1994), 'The Environmental Effects of Trade in the Transport Sector', in: OECD (1994), 153–73.

Laplante, B. and J. Garbalt (1992), 'Environmental Protectionism', *Land Economics*, **68**, 116–19.

Leidy, M. (1994), 'Trade Policy and Indirect Rent Seeking: A Synthesis of Recent Work', *Economics and Politics*, **6**, 97–118.

Leidy, M. and B. Hoekman (1994), '"Cleaning Up" While Cleaning Up: Pollution Abatement, Interest Groups and Contingent Trade Policies', *Public Choice*, **78**, 241–58.

Leonard, H. (1984), *Are Environmental Regulations Driving US Industries Overseas?*, Washington, DC, Conservation Foundation.

Leonard, H. (1988), *Pollution and the Struggle for the World Product*, New York, Cambridge University Press.

Long, N. van and H. Siebert (1991), 'Institutional Competition versus ex-ante Harmonization: The Case of Environmental Policy', *Journal of Institutional and Theoretical Economics*, **147**, 296–311.

López, R. (1994), 'The Environment as a Factor of Production: The Effects of Economic Growth and Trade Liberalization', *Journal of Environmental Economics and Management*, **27**, 163–84.

López, R. (1995), 'The Tragedy of the Commons in Côte d'Ivoire Agriculture: Empirical Evidence and Implications for Trade Policies', University of Maryland at College Park, manuscript.

López, R. (1998), 'Environmental Externalities in Traditional Agriculture and the Impact of Trade Liberalization: The Case of Ghana', *Journal of Development Economics*, forthcoming.

Low, P. (ed.) (1992a), 'International Trade and the Environment', World Bank Discussion Paper No. 159, Washington, DC, World Bank.

Low, P. (1992b), 'Trade Measures and Environmental Quality: The Implications for Mexico's Exports', in: Low (ed.) (1992a), 105–20.

Low, P. and A. Yeats (1992), 'Do Dirty Industries Migrate?', in: Low (1992a), 89–104.

Lucas, R., D. Wheeler and H. Hettige (1992), 'Economic Development, Environmental Regulation and the International Migration of Toxic Industrial Pollution: 1960–88', in: Low (ed.) (1992a), 67–86.

Ludema, R. and I. Wooton (1994), 'Cross-border Externalities and Trade Liberalization: The Strategic Control of Pollution', *Canadian Journal of Economics*, **27**, 950–66.

Lutz, E. (1992), 'Agricultural Trade Liberalization, Price Changes and Environmental Effects', *Environmental and Resource Economics*, **2**, 79–89.

Madeley, J. (1992), *Trade and the Poor*, London, Intermediate Technology Publications.

Magee, S. (1980), 'Three Simple Tests of the Stolper–Samuelson Theorem', in: P. Oppenheimer (ed.), *Issues in International Economics*, Oriel, Stockfield, 138–53.

Maloney, M. and R. McCormick (1982), 'A Positive Theory of Environmental Quality Regulation', *Journal of Law and Economics*, **25**, 99–123.

Markusen, J., E. Morey and N. Olewiler (1993), 'Environmental Policy when Market Structure and Plant Locations are Endogenous', *Journal of Environmental Economics and Management*, **24**, 69–86.

Markusen, J., E. Morey and N. Olewiler (1995), 'Competition in Regional Environmental Policies when Plant Locations are Endogenous', *Journal of Public Economics*, **56**, 55–77.

Mayer, W. (1984), 'Endogenous Tariff Formation', *American Economic Review*, **74/5**, 970–85.

McConnell, V. and R. Schwab (1990), 'The Impact of Environmental Regulation on Industry Location Decisions: The Motor Vehicle Industry', *Land Economics*, **66**, 67–81.

McGuire, M. (1982), 'Regulation, Factor Rewards and International Trade', *Journal of Public Economics*, **17**, 335–54.

Merryfield, J. (1988), 'The Impact of Selected Abatement Strategies on Transnational Pollution, the Terms-of-trade, and Factor Rewards: A General Equilibrium Approach', *Journal of Environmental Economics and Management*, **15**, 259–84.

Motta, M. and J.-F. Thisse (1994), 'Does Environmental Dumping Lead to Delocation?', *European Economic Review*, **38**, 563–76.

Mueller, D. (1989), *Public Choice II*, New York, Cambridge University Press.

Munasinghe, M. and W. Cruz (1995), 'Economywide Policies and the Environment', World Bank Environment Paper No. 10, Washington, DC, World Bank.

Mussa, M. (1982), 'Imperfect Factor Mobility and the Distribution of Income', *Journal of International Economics*, **12**, 125–41.

Oates, W. and R. Schwab (1988), 'Economic Competition Among Jurisdictions: Efficiency Enhancing or Distortion Inducing?', *Journal of Public Economics*, **35**, 333–54.

OECD (1994), *The Environmental Effects of Trade*, Paris, Organization of Economic Cooperation and Development.

OECD (1995), 'Trade, Environment and Development Cooperation', Working Paper No. 45, Paris, Organization of Economic Cooperation and Development.

Olson, M. (1965), *The Logic of Collective Action*, Cambridge, MA, Harvard University Press.

Peirce, W. (1991), 'Unanimous Decisions in a Redistributive Context: The Council of Ministers of the European Communities', in: R. Vaubel and T. Willett (eds), *The Political Economy of International Organization: A Public Choice Approach*, Boulder, CO, Westview Press, 267–85.

Peltzman, S. (1976), 'Toward a More General Theory of Regulation', *Journal of Law and Economics*, **19**, 211–40.

Perroni, C. and R.M. Wigle (1994), 'International Trade and Environmental Quality: How Important are the Linkages?', *Canadian Journal of Economics*, **27**, 551–67.

Pethig, R. (1975), 'Pollution, Welfare, and Environmental Policy in the Theory of Comparative Advantage', *Journal of Environmental Economics and Management*, **2**, 160–69.

Pflüger, M. (1996), 'Ecological Dumping in a General Equilibrium Model with Regional Externalities and Monopolistically Competitive Firms', University of Freiburg, Institut für Allgemeine Wirtschaftsforschung, manuscript.

Pollock Shea, C. (1993), 'European Environmental Policy: Effects of the Single Market', *International Environmental Reporter*, January 13, 30–34.

Pritchett, L. (1996), 'Measuring Outward Orientation in LDCs: Can it be Done?', *Journal of Development Economics*, **49**, 307–35.

Rauscher, M. (1991a), 'Foreign Trade and the Environment', in: Siebert (ed.) (1991), 17–31.

Rauscher, M. (1991b), 'National Environmental Policies and the Effects of Economic Integration', *European Journal of Political Economy*, **7**, 313–29.

Rauscher, M. (1992), 'Economic Integration and the Environment: Effects of Members and Non-members', *Environmental and Resource Economics*, **1**, 221–36.

Rauscher, M. (1994), 'On Ecological Dumping', *Oxford Economic Papers*, **46**, 822–40.

Rauscher, M. (1995), 'Environmental Legislation as a Tool of Trade Policy', in: B. Boero and Z. Silberston (eds), *Proceedings of the 1993 Conference on Environmental Economics*, Macmillan, forthcoming.

Rauscher, M. (1996), 'Environmental Regulation and International Capital Allocation', in: K.-G. Mäler (ed.), *International Environmental Problems: An Economic Perspective*, Amsterdam, Kluwer, forthcoming.

Repetto, R. (1989), 'Economic Incentives for Sustainable Production', in: G. Schramm and J. Warford (eds), *Environmental Management and Economic Development*, Baltimore, MD, Johns Hopkins University Press.

Repetto, R. (1994), *Trade and Sustainable Development*, Environmental and Trade Series No. 1, Geneva, United Nations Environmental Programme.

Robison, H. (1985), 'Who Pays for Industrial Pollution Abatement?', *Review of Economics and Statistics*, **67**, 702–6.

Robison, H. (1988), 'Industrial Pollution Abatement: The Impact on the Balance of Trade', *Canadian Journal of Economics*, **21**, 187–99.

Rodrik, D. (1995), 'Political Economy of Trade Policy', in: G. Grossman (ed.), *Handbook of International Economics*, Vol. 3, 1457–94.

Røpke, I. (1994), 'Trade, Development and Sustainability – A Critical Assessment of the "Free Trade Dogma"', *Ecological Economics*, **9**, 13–22.

Ruffin, R. and R. Jones (1977), 'Protection and Real Wages: The Neoclassical Ambiguity', *Journal of Economic Theory*, **14**, 337–48.

Runge, C.F. (1990), 'Trade Protectionism and Environmental Regulations: The New Non-tariff Barriers', *Northwestern Journal of International Law and Business*, **11**, 47–61.

Runge, C.F. (1993), 'Trade Liberalization and Environmental Quality in Agriculture', *International Environmental Affairs*, **5**, 95–128.

Runge, C.F. (1994), 'The Environmental Effects of Trade in the Agricultural Sector', in: OECD (1994), 19–54.

Salinas-León, R. (1993), 'Green Herrings, NAFTA and the Environment', *Regulation*, **16**, 29–34.

Salop, S. and D. Scheffman (1983), 'Raising Rivals' Cost', *American Economic Review*, **73**, 267–71.

Schuknecht, L. (1992), *Trade Protection in the European Community*, Chur, Harwood Academic Publishers.

Schulze, G.G. (1996), 'Capital Export, Unemployment and Illegal Immigration', CEPR Discussion Paper No. 1394, London, Centre of Economic Policy Research.

Schulze, G.G. (1998), *The Political Economy of Capital Controls*, New York, Cambridge University Press, forthcoming.

Schulze G.G. and H.W. Ursprung (1997), 'Environmental Policy in an Integrated World Economy', University of Konstanz, Department of Economics, manuscript.

Schweinberger, A. (1997), 'Environmental Policies, Comparative Advantage and the Gains/Losses from International Trade', *Japanese Economic Review*, **48**, 199–212.

Selden, T. and D. Song (1994), 'Environmental Quality and Development: Is There a Kuznets Curve for Air Pollution?', *Journal of Environmental Economics and Management*, **27**, 147–62.

Sen, S. (1994), 'The Environmental Effects of Trade in the Fisheries Sector', in: OECD (1994), 103–22.

Shafik, N. and S. Bandyopadhyay (1992), 'Economic Growth and Environmental Quality: Times Series and Cross-Country Evidence', World Bank Policy Research Working Paper No. 904, Washington, DC, World Bank.

Shrybman, S. (1990), 'International Trade and the Environment: An Environmental Assessment of the General Agreement on Tariffs and Trade', *The Ecologist*, **20**, 30–34.

Siebert, H. (ed.) (1991), *Environmental Scarcity: The International Dimension*, Tübingen, Mohr.

Siebert, H. (1995), *The Economics of the Environment*, 4th edn., Berlin, Springer.

Siebert, H. (1998), 'Trade Policy and Environmental Protection', *World Economy*, forthcoming.

Siebert, H., J. Eichberger, R. Gronych and R. Pethig (1980), *Trade and Environment: A Theoretical Inquiry*, Amsterdam, Elsevier.

Smil, V. (1984), *The Bad Earth: Environmental Degradation in China*, London.

Staehelin-Witt, E. and H. Blöchliger (1990), 'Die Umweltzentralbank als Instrument langfristiger Umweltpolitik', *Neue Zürcher Zeitung*, November, 17/18.

Stigler, G. (1971), 'The Theory of Economic Regulation', *Bell Journal of Economics and Management Science*, **2**, 3–21.

Stryker, J. et al. (1989), 'Linkages between Policy Reform and Natural Resource Management in Sub-Saharan Africa', Tufts University, manuscript.

Subramanian, A. (1992), 'Trade Measures for the Environment: A Nearly Empty Box?', *World Economy*, **15**, 132–52.

Task Force on the Environment and the Internal Market (1990), *1992: The Environmental Dimension*, Bonn, Economica.

Thomas, C. and G. Tereposky (1993), 'The NAFTA and the Side Agreement on Environmental Cooperation', *Journal of World Trade Law*, **27**, 5–34.

Tobey, J. (1990), 'The Effects of Domestic Environmental Policies on Patterns of World Trade: An Empirical Test', *Kyklos*, **43**, 191–209.

Ulph, A. (1992), 'The Choice of Environmental Policy Instruments and Strategic International Trade', in: R. Pethig (ed.), *Conflicts and Cooperation in Managing Environmental Resources*, Berlin, Springer, 111–29.

Ulph, A. (1996a), 'Environmental Policy and International Trade when Governments and Producers Act Strategically', *Journal of Environmental Economics and Management*, **30**, 265–81.

Ulph. A. (1996b), 'Strategic Environmental Policy, International Trade and the Single European Market', in: J. Braden, H. Folmer, and T. Ulen (eds), *Environmental Policy with Political and Economical Integration*, Cheltenham, Edward Elgar, 235–58.

Ulph, D. (1994), 'Strategic Innovation and Strategic Environmental Policy', in: Carraro (ed.) (1994), 205–28.

UNCTAD (1995), *Trade, Environment and Development, Lessons from Empirical Studies: The Case of Columbia*, Synthesis Report Prepared for the UNCTAD Secretariat, Geneva, United Nations Conference on Trade and Development.

UNEP (1995), *Economic Policy Reforms and the Environment: African Experiences*, Geneva, United Nations Environmental Programme.

Ursprung, H.W. (1991), 'Economic Policies and Political Competition', in: A. Hillman (ed.), *Markets and Politicians*, Dortrecht, Kluwer, 1–25.

Ursprung, H.W. (1992), 'The Political Economy of Environmental Decision Making', Working Paper Series II, No. 176, University of Konstanz, Department of Economics.

US Department of Commerce (1988), *Manufacturers' Pollution Abatement Capital Expenditures and Operating Costs, Annual Survey of Manufacturers 1988*, Washington, DC, US Department of Commerce, Bureau of Census.

US Department of Commerce (1993), *Pollution Abatement Costs and Expenditures, 1991*, Economics and Statistics Administration, Bureau of the Census, Washington, DC, Government Printing Office.

US Environmental Protection Agency (1996), *Toxic Release Inventories 1992–94*, Washington, DC, Government Printing Office.

Vaubel, R. (1994), 'The Political Economic Analysis of European Integration – A Survey', *European Journal of Political Economy*, **10**, 227–49.

Vogel, D. (1995), *Trading Up: Consumer and Environmental Regulation in a Global Economy*, Cambridge, MA, Harvard University Press.

Voss, G. (1993), *Umweltschutz und Industriestandort*, Köln, Institut der Deutschen Wirtschaft.

Walter, I. (1973), 'The Pollution Content of American Trade', *Western Economic Journal*, **11**, 61–70.

Walter, I. (1982), 'International Economic Repercussions of Environmental Policy: An Economist's Perspective', in: S. Rubin and T. Graham (eds), *Environment and Trade*, Totowa, NJ, Allanheld, Osmun & Co, 22–45.

Weck-Hannemann, H. (1992), *Politische Ökonomie des Protektionismus*, Frankfurt, Campus Verlag.

Weck-Hannemann, H. (1994), 'Die Politische Ökonomie der Umweltpolitik', in: R. Bartel and F. Hackl (eds), *Einführung in die Umweltpolitik*, Munich, Vahlen, 101–17.

Weintraub, S. (1992a), 'US–Mexico Free Trade: Implications for the United States', *Journal of Interamerican Studies and World Affairs*, **34**, 29–52.

Weintraub, S. (1992b), 'Modeling the Industrial Effects of NAFTA', in: Lustig et al. (eds), *North American Free Trade: Assessing the Impact*, Washington, DC, Brookings Institution, 109–43.

Whalley, J. (1996), 'Trade and Environment Beyond Singapore', NBER Working Paper No. 5768, Cambridge, MA, National Bureau of Economic Research.

Wheeler, D. and P. Martin (1992), 'Prices, Policies and the International Diffusion of Clean Technology: The Case of Wood Pulp Production', in: Low (ed.) (1992a), 197–224.

World Bank (1992), *Development and the Environment, World Development Report 1992*, New York, Oxford University Press.

World Bank (1994), *Thailand: Mitigating Pollution and Congestion Impacts in a High-Growth Economy*, Country Economic Report, Washington, DC, World Bank.

WTO (1995a), 'Environmental Benefits of Removing Trade Restrictions and Distortions', Note by the Secretariat, WT/CTE/W/1, Geneva, World Trade Organization.

WTO (1995b), *Trade Policy Review: Thailand 1995*, Geneva, World Trade Organization.

Yohe, G. (1979), 'The Backward Incidence of Pollution Control – Some Comparative Statics in General Equilibrium', *Journal of Environmental Economics and Management*, **6**, 187–98.

Young, M.D. (1994), 'Ecologically-accelerated Trade Liberalisation: A Set of Disciplines for Environment and Trade Agreements', *Ecological Economics*, **9**, 43–51.

Index